The
Sacred
ORDINARY

The
Sacred
ORDINARY

EMBRACING THE HOLY
IN THE EVERYDAY

Leigh McLeroy

LUCIDBOOKS

The Sacred Ordinary

© 2010 by Leigh McLeroy

Published by Lucid Books in Brenham, TX.
    www.LucidBooks.net

First Printing 2010

ISBN-13: 9781935909019
ISBN-10: 1935909010

Special Sales: Most Lucid Books titles are available in special quantity discounts. Custom imprinting or excerpting can also be done to fit special needs. Contact

Lucid Books at info@lucidbooks.net.

Contents

Acknowledgments 9
Introduction 11

Part 1   Ordinary Places

Inside the Junk Drawer 14
Never Closed, Never without a Customer 16
The Waiting Place 18
Seeing Jesus at Bethlehem 19
Bliss in Transit 21
At the Pony League Game 23
Growing into My Grace Clothes 26
"Doing Time" in County 28
Repaired *and* Polished? 30
Wilderness Gardens 31
Grace on Broadway 33
Lordship on Highway 59 35
Stranded, Stuck, or Delayed? 37
Beautiful Interior 39
School Days 42
Comfortably Incarcerated 44
Conformed or Transformed? 46
Fridays at Avalon 48
My Beautiful Desert 50
Six A.M. Saxophone 51
Ant Street Expectations 53
Right Track, Wrong Train 55

Part 2   Ordinary People

Ten Fingers and Ten Toes 60
Who Is My Neighbor? 62
Con Affetto, Please 64
A Hero in the Wings 66
The Kindness of Strangers 68
The Balcony Dancer 70
Spending It All 72
Tsunami Baby 74
Sweet Sixty-five 76
Miss Laura's Mail 78

79 A Midweek Deli Drama
81 Night (and Day)
83 Pomp and Circumstance
85 Death Defeated!
87 God's Work and Good Tables
89 "Daddy's Got You!"
91 Of Spiderman and Kings
93 The Things That Julia Moves
95 Horse Holders, Handlers, and Other Hangers-on
97 Written on Her Forehead
99 "My Name Is Dulcinea"
100 No-Matter-What Love

Part 3   Ordinary Things

104 Awaiting New Wine
106 "Six-Foot Frosty Seeks Same . . ."
107 Sanctification and Bathroom Rugs
109 The Problem with Paper Gowns
111 My Window Malfunction
113 Not a Sparrow Falls
115 The Stereographic View
117 Sixty-four-Crayon Life!
119 The Catalog Life
121 About Those Expiration Dates . . .
122 Finding Feathers
124 Finding (More) Feathers
126 King of Hearts
128 Bargain-Basement Deals
130 Any Tree That Isn't Mine
132 Missing Pieces
134 The One-Eyed Tiger
136 God's "iPod-ness"
138 Respecting the Storm
140 Considering Monovision
142 No Hope—or New Hope?
144 Loving the Weight of the Wood

Part 4   Ordinary Moments

148 Changing the Porch Light
149 Caught!
151 Shine
153 Lost Ticket
155 Extra-Inning Exhaustion
157 Where's Your Treasure?
159 Dinner for Two (Plus Two)

Living with My Hands Full 161
The Bread and the Wine Came to Me 163
Don't Supersize Me! 165
Called to Small 167
The Loveliest Ruins 169
Working around the Repairs 170
Sounding Out the Words 172
When Chester Smiled 174
Wrestling the Tree 176
Turbulence 178
Sealed with a Kiss 180
A Freakish Storm 182
Watch This! Watch This! 184
Just Dessert 186
Passing by the Dragon 188
Face Time 190
Keeping Score 192

Part 5   Ordinary Words

Why? 196
"Two Ticks. No Dog." 197
"Tale as Old as Time, Song as Old as Rhyme" 199
Dependence Day 201
This Is My Father's World 203
Love beyond Degree 205
The Determined Hound of Heaven 207
"I See the Moon" 209
He's Just *That* Into You" 211
From the Mouths of Rock Stars 213
Of Football and Messiahs 215
Only Words 217
"It's about the Movie" 219
"Can You Hear Me Now?" 221
Embraceable Inconsistencies 223
God in the Details 225
God Is Love 226
"The Good Kind of Cry" 228
When the Answer Is "No" 230
The Three That Count 231
Worlds Away 233
Weakness before Wonder 235

Personal Retreat Guide 239
Notes 250

Acknowledgments

Thank you to the small circle of family and friends who six years ago said they'd be glad to receive a few words from me each week about what I see God doing in my world. That reading circle has taken on a life of its own as I email five hundred or so words to upwards of a thousand folks . . . and they pass them on. Many recipients of these "Wednesday words" write back, sharing their own observations in response. It feels a little like a secret club of observers, and I'm thankful that our dialogue has lasted so long. The devotional pieces in this book are the result of hundreds of Wednesdays, watching for God at work, listening for his whisper, waiting for his touch. He never fails to meet me in my ordinary days.

Thank you to my family, for your steadying love. Thank you to my City of Refuge family, for sweet community. Thank you Lee, for tutoring me in the ways of "book world." Thank *you*, for buying and reading this book. (Tell someone else about it when you're done, will you?)

Thank you, Jesus. You're everything to me.

Introduction

"Earth's crammed with heaven," wrote Elizabeth Barrett Browning, "and every common bush afire with God—but only he who sees takes off his shoes."

I mean to be one who sees. One who watches for crepe myrtles to combust, expecting now and then to spy heaven hidden in the mundane. And it happens. The question is whether anyone will notice when it does.

Many people assume God wound this world up like a clock and walked away as it began to tick.

I am not among them.

I believe he is active and evident in our everyday goings-on—and that part of my assignment is to discover where and how. It's this kind of wide-awake living that *The Sacred Ordinary* explores. And it's not just my exclusive perspective. You can know it too.

Jesus had a way of making ordinary water pots vessels of wonder, of working blazing miracles in mud. He told simple stories of lost coins and full barns and hungry neighbors and rebellious sons—and his everyday stories rang with sacred truth. He mixed it up with sinners and strugglers and rubbed shoulders with "the locals" everywhere he went. He saw things. He changed things.

By sharing what I see in ordinary things, places, people, moments, and words, I'm hoping to entice you to begin looking for God in your own corner of the world. Because the kingdom of heaven really *is* nearer than you think, even today.

Part *1*

Ordinary
Places

Inside the Junk Drawer

*M*ost folks I know have a junk drawer, and I'm no different from most folks. The first drawer closest to the kitchen door is the designated one—and not long ago, the drawer refused to open. At first I ignored this minor inconvenience, but in a short time I realized that although the contents of my junk drawer are a random assemblage of uncategorized stuff, I open it quite a lot. Because you never know: that odd thing I'm looking for just *might* be tucked inside.

When the unavailable contents of my junk drawer began to torment me, I stuck my head underneath the cabinet to see if I could fix the jam. The drawer had simply fallen off its "track," and needed to be pulled completely out and set right again. Doing so took a while, but when I finally succeeded I decided there was no better time than the present to take an inventory of my junk. Everything was in full view with the drawer pulled out—even the stuff I hadn't seen in years.

Stuff like a new deck of airline playing cards, cellophane wrapper still intact. A half-used roll of silver duct tape. A few petrified pieces of Halloween candy, year of origin unknown. My dog's first tiny puppy collar, just big enough for my own wrist. A Polaroid photo of an old friend and me, taken in a room I didn't recognize. Three glue sticks, all new. Snippets of Christmas ribbon and two packages of dark brown shoestrings. (I don't own any dark brown lace-ups.)

As far as I could see, these random items had only one thing in common: I didn't *need* any of them, but at some point, I hadn't been able to throw them away.

My heart has a junk drawer too. And I wish *it* would get stuck more often.

I visit it when I'm searching for reasons why God shouldn't love me. When I'm feeling lonely or useless or discouraged. And in it I find odd pieces of my own history that shouldn't matter anymore but still do—some far older than a few candy pieces gone bad. This heart-drawer holds secret sins, confessed—forgiven!—but not yet removed from my memory's outtake reel. Words I wish I'd never spoken. Words I wish I had. Failures. Lapses in ordinary kindness. Moments of misplaced shame. Old hurts I still pick the scabs from. Scars I like too much.

This junk has been forgiven, or redeemed, or transformed—but still I hold on. It's trash. All of it. So the next time this drawer hesitates to open, I mean to let it stay shut. If God has forgotten its contents, then by his mercy I can too.

> Formerly, when you did not know God, you were slaves to those who by nature are not gods. But now that you know God—or rather are known by God—how is it that you are turning back to those weak and miserable principles? Do you wish to be enslaved by them all over again?
>
> Galatians 4:8–9 NIV

If your heart's junk drawer is crammed full too, wouldn't this be a fine day to begin to empty it out completely? Where would you choose to start?

Never Closed,
Never without a Customer

The "original" Original Pantry in downtown Los Angeles opened in 1924 and has been open every day since. When the first location was vacated in 1950 to make room for a freeway off-ramp, the short-order cooks, busboys, waiters, and waitresses finished with the lunch crowd, then moved one block east to serve dinner at the "new" location on the corner of South Figueroa and 9th Street, where the Pantry sits today.

Clark Gable was a regular back in the day, and as the story goes, Mikhail Baryshnikov and Lucille Ball once ate there at the same time, although at different tables.

Eighty-seven customers can be served at once; that's two thousand plus each day. On the morning I stopped in, the cast included three parrot-headed punkers who had probably not yet been to bed, a well-dressed, middle-aged couple in a silent standoff over their eggs, and a filthy woman at the bar who barked at herself over the din of clanging dishes.

Their coffee cups kept getting filled, just like mine did—and the food kept coming out of the kitchen, one heaping platter at a time. I watched and was reminded that grace is a meal, taken over and over, made possible by a single, once-and-for-all payment. It's served up in a place that never closes, for an odd collection of humanity that always changes, with a constant supply of nourishment that never ceases. No star treatment for anyone. The same unblinking, evenhanded service for everyone. The oddest tablemates imaginable. And the smoke coming off the grill filling the dining hall with the smell of sustenance and soot.

Never closed, never without a customer. Isn't that just like the mercy seat of God?

At the cashier's cage near the door of the Pantry, everyone—rich, poor, famous, nameless—pays his tab. The floor before the cage is worn down from the shifting feet of so many diners, exposing layer upon layer of dirty linoleum.

Still, I wouldn't have been surprised if the cashier in the hooded sweatshirt had smiled at me and said, "No charge, honey. Yours is already covered."

Why? Because I'm told that "by one offering He has perfected for all time those who are sanctified. And the Holy Spirit also testifies to us; for after saying, 'This is the covenant that I will make with them after those days, says the Lord: I will put My laws upon their heart, and on their mind I will write them,' He then says, 'And their sins and their lawless deeds I will remember no more'" (Heb. 10:14–17).

Now where there is forgiveness of these things, there is no longer any offering needed for sin.

Alleluia and amen.

What does it mean to you that God's mercy seat never "closes?" How will you honor him today for paying your tab forever?

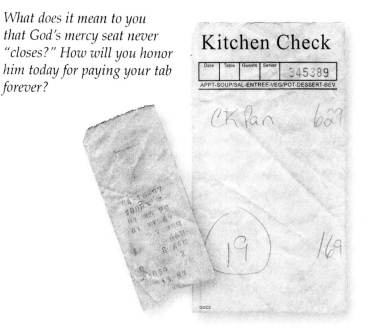

Kitchen Check

The Waiting Place

I once recorded a bit of Dr. Seuss's *Oh, the Places You'll Go* on my home voice mail. It was a clever bit about "the waiting place . . . where everyone is just waiting. For a train to go or a bus to come, or plane to go or the mail to come . . . or a phone to ring or the snow to snow . . . just . . . waiting."[1]

I liked the message a lot. But after the first time or two, hardly anyone who called enjoyed sitting through "the waiting place." Because the truth is, waiting rather quickly loses whatever charm it might have had early on. Even so, I know very few people who are not—at any given time—waiting for something. To receive test results, perhaps. Or to reach the front of the checkout line. To welcome home a loved one. To hear their name called on a try-out list. To be asked to marry, or to dance. To see a stoplight (or a season) change. To hold a baby in their arms.

Like it or not, we all do time in the waiting place. The question is, will we do anything of value *with* that time? Do we simply languish until our circumstances change— or are we willing to linger in discomfort, and learn while we wait?

The Bible is full of wait-ers. Sarai. Elizabeth. Hannah. Moses. David. Hosea. Jonah. Job. What might we have heard if their voices had been recorded? "It's no use. I'll never have a child." Or, "Why shouldn't I be stuck with someone else's sheep for the rest of my life? I'm a murderer. I'm no good for anything else." Or, "Samuel must have been mistaken when he anointed me king. Saul will kill me before he lets me take his throne."

Some wait-ers *did* wallow in self-doubt and pity . . . for a while. But more often than not, these God-followers learned to linger in their waiting places, seeing all that there was to see. And what there usually was to see was evidence of a great, patient, provident God at work—in the smallest of circumstances and in the hidden places of the human heart.

A wise friend told me once that we are never alone in the cold, dim cave of uncertainty. When our eyes adjust to the half-light, he said, we will see that there are tens, hundreds, thousands, even—waiting with us. And maybe, he said, waiting for a word *from* us that injects hope or humor or sense into what seems to make no sense at all.

Are you waiting? Me too. Here's a meantime word for us both:

> Do you not know? Have you not heard? The Everlasting God, the LORD, the Creator of the ends of earth does not become weary or tired. His understanding is inscrutable. He gives strength to the weary, and to him who lacks might He increases power . . . those who wait for the LORD will gain new strength.
>
> Isaiah 40:28–29, 31

What good use could be made of your waiting time? Pray for God's strength to infuse your weariness—and for his power to supply your might. He has not grown tired in your waiting place, and he is the one who is holding you.

Seeing Jesus at Bethlehem

German immigrants built the Bethlehem Lutheran Church in Round Top, Texas, in 1866, and it's still standing. Carl Bauer and his two sons and sons-in-law set much of the native limestone in place, and they are buried in the adjoining cemetery, near the irrefutable proof of their good workmanship. Civil War service markers top both sons' graves.

Once, on a beautiful spring afternoon, a friend and I drove west from Houston to Sealy, New Ulm, Industry, and Round Top, and stopped by Bethlehem Lutheran before ducking into Royer's Café for lunch. The church was empty except for the two of us, and so we wandered up and down the aisles, admiring the old building's quaint simplicity. Ceiling fans hung still over empty pews, and a large Bible lay open on the altar. The communion vessels stood to one side, covered with linen and old lace. A dark, faded picture of Christ hung between the altar and the high, narrow window above it.

I could not stand inside Bethlehem for long without imagining the weddings, funerals, revivals, baptisms, and blessings that must have taken place there in the nearly 150 years since the Bauer men had finished their good work.

On the way out we stopped to sign the open guestbook near the foyer door. My friend signed first, then me. As I glanced up from the book, I noticed a Xeroxed sheet of paper posted in front of me. "Instructions for Ushers" it said, and an item near the bottom of the list caught my eye.

"Unplug the Jesus picture," it read.

I motioned my friend over, and we both howled with laughter. Thinking if "unplugging" was listed, there had to be an earlier "plug in" instruction, I scanned higher on the list. There it was. Item 2: "Plug in the Jesus picture at the altar."

We walked to the front of the church again, and my friend disappeared behind the faded picture we'd barely noticed before. Seconds later, the image was illuminated from behind. He was instantly beautiful. His glowing face made the whole room seem warmer. Jesus's eyes were deep brown, and his robe was blue. One elegant hand was raised to his chest.

We were nearly back to Houston before the plain truth hit my heart: *Isn't that just what we do?* We faithfully "plug in" Jesus each week when we arrive at church and just as faithfully unplug him when we leave. But what he means for us to do is let his image shine forth from his true dwelling place—us!—all the time.

How do I know? Because he said so:

> You are the light of the world. A city set on a hill cannot be hidden; nor does anyone light a lamp and put it under a basket, but on the lampstand, and it gives light to all who are in the house. Let your light shine before men in such a way that they may see your good works, and glorify your Father who is in heaven.
>
> Matthew 5:14–16

Break the ushers' rules. Let the light of Jesus keep shining, even when his church house is empty, because your heart never is.

Bliss in Transit

The eastbound Max train from Pioneer Square runs all the way to the Portland, Oregon, airport—and on the day I rode, the train was not crowded. Just me, a youngish couple to my right, two guys farther up with their bags near their feet and their cell phones holstered like six shooters, one lone eastbound commuter, and a woman with a baby stroller. No one spoke above a whisper. Until Bliss boarded.

The kid wore a baggy T-shirt and pants he appeared to be in imminent danger of losing. His head was shaved and his feet were dirty. He strode confidently into the car, and I quickly looked down to avoid eye contact. I could see the hustle coming. He zeroed in instead on the couple next to me, extended his hand, and said "Hey, man, I'm Bliss—where are you guys from?"

"New York," the male half of the couple said, and Bliss seemed to like that.

"Cool, you're from the city," he countered. Then his monologue began. He was a musician, he explained, and maybe they'd caught his band a month or so ago on an MTV special, or heard him on the local indie station. He and his buddies had put some new songs together and needed funds to cut a demo. Not your normal panhandler, I decided. This one's got a story—and he plans to tell it.

"I don't want to just ask you for a buck or something," Bliss explained. "Everyone does that. I want to make something for you."

Now I was curious. Balloon animals? A quick macramé key chain?

"I'm gonna make you a rhyme," he said. "It's a good rhyme I've been workin' on—and I think you're gonna like it."

New York guy must have reached into his pocket to give Bliss a buck in exchange for silence, but he declined any payment until full services were rendered. "Just wait, man," he said. "And if you think it's cool, then we're even."

He steadied himself in the center of the car and then started his rap/beat poem about himself and his music. His voice was loud and clear. He did not look down once, although the rest of us did a time or two. He used one

22

off-color slang word and then half apologized: "Sorry to offend, man, but this is art."

When he finished the poem, Bliss took the dollar re-extended to him—but instead of slinking away, he looked his newest benefactor square in the eye: "So, did you like it? I hope you liked it. Was it better than you expected it would be?"

Bliss was hustling for money. No doubt about that. But he was clearly a man who loved his work. And as he exited at the next stop, it occurred to me that he was less reticent to sell his unspectacular words than I usually am to *give away* my extraordinary faith. What I have to offer is priceless—but it can be had for less than a buck. And I know without asking that it's better than good.

So why am I not just as willing to put it on the line—anywhere, anytime—the way Bliss was, in transit?

> For I am not ashamed of the gospel, for it is the power of God for salvation to everyone who believes . . . for in it the righteousness of God is revealed.
>
> Romans 1:16–17

Truthfully, sometimes I am ashamed—not of the gospel itself, but of my halfhearted effort to offer it up freely to a world that waits, dying to hear. The list of lesser things I'm more ready to share with others is simply too long. What about yours?

At the Pony League Game

The last time I saw the Padres play they lost 12–8. No, not the San Diego Padres . . . the Post Oak Pony League

Padres. But every time I see them play they remind me why I love Pony League ball: these kids are most decidedly *not* professionals.

Anything can happen when nine thirteen-year-old boys take the field. A fielder can decide a hard-hit grounder looks a little too wicked to stop and nimbly jump out of its way. A wild-as-a-March-hare pitcher one inning can strike out three in a row with ten pitches the next. And a kid who just whiffed for his team's third out can tear down to first base, beat the sleeping catcher's throw, and keep the inning alive.

Winners can whoop it up, losers can pout, and moms can wait behind the dugout when the game is over and ask their sons—fresh from battle—if they remembered their bat and glove.

The game is not neat. It's not predictable. It's a whole lot like life.

Unlike Pony leaguers, professionals are more consumed with outcome than process. They don't have much fun at all unless they win—and they prefer to win big. They'd rather be caught dead than cry over a losing effort, because professionals are all about scoring, saving face, and maintaining tight control.

The trouble is, you never really win that way.

Listen to these words from a guy widely considered to be a big-timer on the preaching circuit, as he explains the way things are in his league: "The foolishness of God is wiser than men, and the weakness of God is stronger than men. For consider your calling, brethren, that there were not many wise according to the flesh, not many mighty, not many noble; but God has chosen the foolish things of the world to shame the wise, and God has chosen the weak things of the world to shame the things which are strong, and the base things of the world and the despised God has chosen, the things that are not, so that He may nullify the things that are" (1 Cor. 1:25–28).

Why would Paul, the big-time evangelist, say such things? Why would he claim that it is the foolish—and not the professional—whom God most readily uses?

Because God would have no man to boast before him. Because our "errors"—our passed balls and wild pitches and fielding hiccups and walked-in runs—keep us humble and prevent us from considering ourselves big league Christ followers.

Aren't we lucky to be unpolished players, all of us? To wear our feelings on our sleeves and commit our goofs in full view of the crowd? To glory in our shining moments but never count on their consistency? To delight in the game but not believe for an instant that we control its twists and turns?

There's a ragtag glory in humility that really does beat all—and only makes the heart beat faster when we hear the words "Play ball!"

Where is the wise? Where is the scribe? Where is the disputer of this age? Has not God made foolish the wisdom of this world?

1 Corinthians 1:20 NKJV

Have you "gone pro" without noticing? Are you so concerned with winning that you've lost the love of playing? Glory in your inconsistency. Celebrate your unpolished skill. Cast your fate with the team and trust God for the outcome. In time you just might learn to love the amateur's game.

Growing into My Grace Clothes

$\mathcal{B}$allinger, Texas, was never a very big town—but when I was a child it seemed a lot bigger. Most of my mother's family lived in this sleepy west-central Texas hamlet at one time or another, making it the default destination of many a childhood road trip.

The most impressive building in Ballinger by far was the Runnels County courthouse, but the center of commerce was comprised of a two- or three-square-block cluster of buildings that locals called not "downtown" but simply "town."

I had two favorite stores in "town." One was Keel Drug, where I drank milk shakes on a twirling stool, bought rolls of Lifesavers with someone else's money, and read and reread every greeting card in stock. The other was a dress shop called Middleton's.

I loved Middleton's. Loved its plaster manikins dressed to the nines in the front window, its spacious, mirrored dressing rooms, and the sprawling back room that opened out to the alley. There next season's clothes hung neatly in fragrant cedar closets, a pot of coffee sat warming all day, and every nook and corner offered a wonderful place to hide.

Owner Anne Middleton had excellent taste, with which she clothed a large percentage of the women in my family, including my grandmother, aunts, and older cousins. But when I began to visit Middleton's I was far too young to wear its clothes. I could disappear into the racks and search the mysteries of the back room to my heart's content—but nothing in the store fit me. I was too small, and the clothes were too big.

I became a Christ follower when I was eight. I was old enough to appreciate that the gift I'd received was rich and fine but not yet mature enough to "fill it out." At eight, I had more opportunity before me than history behind me. I had only experienced a hint of the riches my God had in store. So I did what I learned to do at Middleton's. I made myself at home in the store and dreamed of the day I'd be big enough to wear some of its finer treasures home.

Today Middleton's is closed. Its main street windows no longer beckon small-town women who enjoy being well dressed. But God's storehouse of grace is still open. And I shop often.

His grace was sufficient at eight, and eighteen, and twenty-eight. It has fit me like a glove at twenty, and thirty, and even forty. It's been all that I've needed, whenever I've needed it. I've never once left his presence empty-handed— and I've never paid. Not because I'm a beggar or a thief, but because he owns the store, and I'm his child. Times and styles will change, but his grace never will. I am still so very glad to be his.

> Therefore, having been justified by faith, we have peace with God through our Lord Jesus Christ, through whom also we have obtained our introduction by faith into this grace in which we stand.
>
> Romans 5:1–2

What a pity to never grow past our introduction to grace! What a waste to only window-shop the riches of his storehouse long after we've grown big enough to wear its clothes! What are you waiting for? Come on in.

"Doing Time" in County

The criminal justice building in my hometown was not a familiar destination for me. I followed the Internet map I'd printed like it led to a foreign country. The procedure for entering the edifice was just as foreign: drop your purse, notebook, and keys on the conveyer belt and step through the metal detector toward a waiting officer. I felt like a rookie and was silently glad for that fact.

Past the entry gauntlet I found the crowded elevator bank and waited through three full cars before I managed to squeeze in for the ride up to court. I shared my personal space with so many visitors, clerks, deputies, handcuffed passengers, and attorneys with files-on-wheels that we must have been very near the posted maximum weight limit.

The courtroom I entered was full too, but the docket was quickly called. I waited for the name I'd come to hear as pleas were made, attorneys appointed, and papers filed. Some there were visibly nervous. The young person I'd come to support was among them. But others wore a bored, "been there, done that" look. I got anxious just watching. (I was sent to the principal's office once . . . in junior high.)

All those required to be in court were there for one reason: they were accused of breaking the law. And alleged lawbreakers must answer their charges in court.

Once the bit of business I'd come for was done, I left the courtroom. Again, a crowd of people waited for the elevator. A man next to me held a sheet of yellow paper. He looked at me with what appeared to be relief and said, "Man, that is *one* scary place. My heart is beating so fast I think I might faint."

"I think they mean for it to be scary," I said.

"I got me thirty days in County," he offered. "Thirty days for some bologna and crackers and cheese." (I didn't ask.)

"Thirty days," he repeated. And he seemed glad that was all. "I'm gonna get me a big old sweater to wear in, so I can take it off and use it for a pillow at night." Another man nearby (also with paperwork) spoke up: "You don't get to pick your clothes, man. They'll be giving you a jumpsuit. Orange."

The elevator arrived, and we all went our separate ways.

The guy with the yellow paper was obviously found guilty, but he was almost giddy with the thought that his punishment (for now, anyway) would be light. And he was inexperienced enough in crime to think that "County" was a much more comfortable, accommodating place than it really is.

That's how sin deceives us. We think we're in better shape than we are—and that prison is a nicer kind of place than it turns out to be. We need to know the truth about slavery to sin, but repeated trips to County won't teach us. Only grace will. Only grace.

> But thanks be to God that though you were slaves of sin, you became obedient from the heart . . . and having been freed from sin, you became slaves of righteousness. . . . For the wages of sin is death, but the free gift of God is eternal life in Christ Jesus our Lord.
>
> Romans 6:17–18, 23

Have you become sin's willing captive? Are you truly comfortable there? Even a nice, clean cell with three square meals a day is still jail. What would it take for you to clasp the hand of the One with the key—and finally be set free?

Repaired *and* Polished?

I visited the shoe repair shop with a ten-year-old pair of black lace-up boots that had died a rather ignoble death due to drowning. An unfortunate pause in a deep puddle had caused the top of one boot near the ball of my foot to pull away from the sole, leaving a yawning gap where plenty of sock showed.

Truth be told, the shoe shop wasn't my initial attempt at repair; I stopped first at my kitchen closet to see what kind of glue I might have to solve the problem without "professional" intervention. (For the record, Elmer's wood glue would not.)

The nice, bespectacled man on the other side of the shop counter eyed my boots and asked me two questions: first, what kind of glue had I used to try to fix the problem myself . . . and then, without acknowledging the idiocy of trying to repair a leather boot with wood glue, whether the next day after 2 p.m. would be all right for pickup.

Evidently my boots were salvageable—in spite of my fears that I had utterly ruined them. As I left, he spoke another question, almost as an afterthought: "Repaired *and* polished?" he asked. That sounded good to me. I nodded yes.

The next afternoon I returned and presented my ticket. The same man-of-few-words disappeared behind some shelves and returned with what looked like my old boots, reborn. Soles attached. Repaired and polished to a shine so new I could almost see myself in the toes. The $18 he charged me seemed ridiculously low.

As I paid, I noticed that someone in front of me had left a pair of work boots so scarred and beat up I wondered why their owner didn't just buy a new pair. The entire sole of one boot was peeled back like the lid of a sardine can, and worn duct tape flapped out from both sides. (Note to self: duct tape might be a temporary fix, but its shoe-repairing efficacy is ultimately no better than wood glue.)

If I hadn't just witnessed my own shoe resurrection, I might have thought those work boots were beyond saving. But my old pair, repaired and polished, made me reconsider. I imagined how delighted the owner of these boots would be in a day or so, and I left the shop thankful that beyond life's wear and tear and futile efforts at self-repair, there's something even more permanent and beautiful available to me:

> Therefore if anyone is in Christ he is a new creature; the old things passed away; behold, new things have come.
>
> 2 Corinthians 5:17

Is there something in your life you believe might be beyond repair? When will you stop trying to remedy it yourself and take it to the One who makes all things new?

Wilderness Gardens

*I*n February of 1942, President Franklin D. Roosevelt signed Executive Order 9066, empowering the United States secretary of war to relocate nearly 120,000 Japanese Americans from their west coast homes to ten "war relocation centers."

I've visited the ruins of one of them.

Manzanar was a one-square-mile encampment that from 1942 to 1945 was home to over 11,000 Japanese men, women, and children. Relocated "detainees" were given a week or less to pack their belongings into two suitcases and close their homes, not knowing when—or if—they would be allowed to return.

Once the camp held thirty-six blocks of wooden barracks, a high school, baseball fields, a hospital, a town hall, and a newspaper office that published the *Manzanar Free Press*. Three Buddhist temples and a Roman Catholic church were constructed, but no hint of them remains. Still faintly discernable, however, are the remnants of elaborate gardens built by the residents to improve the barren landscape. Ponds were dug. Rocks were moved and re-erected in symmetrical patterns. And green things grew. In the midst of sorrow, there was beauty.

Manzanar's ruins were haunting. Ghostly. Sad. But it was not the flat, ruined landscape that I couldn't shake. It was imagining the green, growing gardens in the midst of it—the way they must have looked more than six decades ago.

Each of us has wilderness times. Times of displacement. Forced exile. Separation from the comforts of home and routine, of family and friends. Hopefully, when they come, something deep in our spirit remembers green and growing things and tries to re-create their beauty, even only temporarily.

For those of us who belong to God there is another dynamic at work. We may *decorate* our barren places, but he himself transforms them in a way that is permanent, and lasting. "Indeed, the LORD will comfort Zion; He will comfort all her waste places. And her wilderness He will make like Eden, and her desert like the garden of the LORD; joy and gladness will be found in her, thanksgiving and sound of a melody" (Isa. 51:3).

In Israel's darkest hours, God said, "I will put the cedar in the wilderness, the acacia and the myrtle and the olive tree; I will place the juniper in the desert together with the box tree and the cypress, that they may see and recognize, and consider and gain insight as well, that the hand of the LORD has done this, and the Holy One of Israel has created it" (Isa. 41:19–20).

If there are fragrant and fruitful trees in my own wilderness (and there are), you can be sure that it is God who has caused them to flower and burst with life.

On the bottom of the National Park Service flyer I stuffed in my bag leaving Manzanar, I found this factoid: "manzanar" means apple orchard. And I guess I should have suspected something like it. I may, in faith, plant trees in my wilderness. But only he can bring forth their fruit.

Have you been forced into a place you never wanted to be? A waste place or wilderness that seems far from home and any true comfort? God knows. In fact, he exiled himself to such a place for your behalf, and there bore for you the life-giving fruit of his own sacrifice. Is it any wonder that he can make anything bloom . . . anywhere?

Grace on Broadway

When my sister and I were very young, we carved our shared initials (both of us were "LM"s) into one of my mother's end tables with a straight pin. Since neither LM would admit who actually did the deed, we both got a pretty solid spanking. That was justice.

Once, in junior high, it snowed in Houston—and I made an icy snowball to throw at a friend who was boarding the school bus. Only I didn't hit him—I hit our assistant principal, Dr. LaForge. The next day he called me to his office, but instead of giving me detention, he teased me that since I played basketball, he thought I'd have been a better shot. And then he laughed and sent me back to class. That was mercy.

From life I've learned what grace is not. It's not exactly justice. And it's not quite mercy, either. But aside from the book of Romans, there's nowhere I've learned more vividly about the true nature of grace than on Broadway. That's right. Broadway.

From *Camelot*, I learned that grace is essential. It's essential because, as with Guinevere, my sin was my own death sentence. My betrayal of the standard required by my king, apart from grace, could have only one outcome: execution. The laws of Camelot demanded that payment for betrayal must be made, and no one could excuse Guinevere's sin but the king himself. For Guinevere to live, Camelot had to die. The reckoning was awful and inevitable. And grace was essential.

From *Les Miserables*, I learned that grace is undeserved. Jean Valjean was imprisoned for theft and released years later with only the clothes on his back and no hope for a better life. Given shelter in the home of a priest, he stole the man's silver and fled in the dark—but he was quickly captured. When the constable brought Valjean before the priest, the kind man insisted that he'd *given* the silver to Valjean and then gave him two remaining candlesticks as well. The first time I saw this scene in a darkened theater I knew that I too had been caught red-handed and gifted in a way I never, ever deserved.

Tell all the Truth but tell it slant—
Success in Circuit lies
Too bright for our infirm Delight
The Truth's superb surprise

As Lightning to the Children eased
With explanation kind
The Truth must dazzle gradually
Or every man be blind—[2]

Emily Dickinson

From *My Fair Lady*, I apprehended the

34

irreversible nature of grace. Training and fine clothes made cockney Eliza Doolittle a fine lady for one unforgettable evening, but at the end of that evening, her street accent (and her anger) returned. Only love made her a lady for life. And once loved by Henry Higgins, Eliza was permanently transformed.

That's grace. It's absolutely essential. Totally underserved. Completely irreversible—and mine! So grace to you too, from God our Father, and the Lord Jesus Christ. (With a little help from Guinevere, Jean Valjean, and Eliza.) There's no place that God cannot speak his truth if we will only open our ears—and our hearts—to hear.

> For it is by grace you have been saved, through faith.
>
> Ephesians 2:8

Jesus must have spun stories because they're sneakier than sermons. They infiltrate our senses and weave their way into our hearts before we see their deeper meaning coming. They tell us the truth, like poet Emily Dickinson said, but tell it slant, because the beautiful, weighty truth really is "too bright for our infirm delight." I'm convinced our Lord is still subversively telling stories. Have you heard a good one lately?

Lordship on Highway 59

I'd traveled this particular stretch of Texas highway before, but with almost ten hours of driving time ahead, there was plenty to see that was new. A fresh carpet of multihued wildflowers drifted wide on either side of me, like forgotten confetti from an early Easter parade. Wobbly calves shadowed their grazing mothers in green fields, and fading billboards advertised small-town places where I'd never stopped.

But the sight that caught my eye and held it on this particular trip was a single sign in front of a simple, red-brick church. I'll call it the "Bluebonnet Believers' Church," even though it wasn't. On this sign, right below the words "Bluebonnet Believers' Church," were the kind of plastic letters you can change from week to week. This week they said, "Where Jesus is Lord."

I was half a mile down the road before it hit me: "Is there anywhere he *isn't*?" Is there a place where Jesus is not Lord—regardless of whether he is acknowledged as such? No. There is not. Because he himself said, "All authority on heaven and earth has been given to me." That about covers the waterfront, doesn't it? Heaven. And earth. All authority.

I know what the good folks at Bluebonnet must have meant. They must have meant where Jesus is *honored* as Lord, or *exalted* as Lord, or worshiped and obeyed as Lord. They were, I think, referring to their particular response to the fact of his lordship, not announcing the precise locality of his rule.

But their sign made me think in a way that was true, even if accidental. It reminded me that God's kingdom is boundless, and his rule extends far, far beyond my ability to proclaim it. "Where Jesus is Lord" reiterated that his lordship is never the thing in question—only my response to it. And that the one place I want to be utterly certain that Jesus is revered and worshiped and obeyed and exalted as the Lord of all life . . . is in mine.

He is the image of the invisible God, the firstborn of all creation. For by Him all things were created, both in the heavens and on earth, visible and invisible, whether thrones or dominions or rulers or authorities—all things have been created through Him and for Him. He is before all things, and in Him all things hold together. He is also the head of the body, the church; and He is the beginning, the firstborn from the dead, so that He Himself will come to have first place in everything.

Colossians 1:15–18

It would be far, far easier to worry about whether Jesus is recognized, revered, and obeyed as Lord in my church, or your church, or the United States Senate, or in my neighborhood, even, than whether Jesus is being recognized, revered, and obeyed as Lord in my own heart and life. But I only have say-so over the latter. His Word says that he is, indeed, Lord of heaven and earth. I believe that. The question that remains is whether I will submit to him as Lord in my life, today.

Stranded, Stuck, or Delayed?

A trip to the Texas hill country for rest and relaxation coincided with the season's heaviest rains, and so for almost thirty-six hours, I was stranded in my retreat hideaway. I stayed in a small house on a high bluff with no telephone, no television, and no radio—a place aptly and affectionately called "The Quiet House." When the river nearby became swift enough for me to hear its rushing over the thunder, and the lights flickered off for the sixth or seventh time, I did something I'd never done before when staying there: I picked up the radio handset, turned it on, and said "Hello . . . anybody there?"

The radio crackled and the camp foreman answered quickly. "Glad you called. We were getting worried about you. The river's closed, and more storms are coming in. Are you safe and dry?" I assured him that I was.

The river was the Frio, and in this beautiful place it juts through a deep canyon and along a limestone bottom, usually covered by six to eight inches of water. In fact, the day I arrived I drove through the riverbed to the camp office to check in. Now it was running over five feet deep.

I was stranded, but I was safe. And although I couldn't leave—I hadn't planned to for another day anyway. So I lit the house's oil lamps, set dry wood in the fireplace, and climbed up into the loft to listen to the river and the rain. Up in the loft, settled into deep, soft cushions and feeling quite content, I saw a squirrel that was more stuck than stranded just a few feet away on the other side of the window. He clung upside down under the eaves of the house, with water coming off the roof in a torrent. It was as if he was under a miniature waterfall twenty feet off the ground and hanging on for dear life. His tiny feet were clamped vise-like to a wet, wooden beam and his drenched tail was too wet to twitch.

Sometimes life strands us. Sometimes it leaves us hopelessly stuck. Sometimes, like Tom Hanks's delightful character Viktor Navorsky in *The Terminal*, we are "delayed." Viktor was detained in a fictional New York City airport because, while en route to that city, his small Eastern European country was overtaken in a coup. Once he landed, Viktor held a passport to a country that no longer existed—and governmental red tape prevented his leaving until those matters were satisfactorily resolved. As a result, he lived in the airport terminal for many days, existing on food court scraps and the kindness of baggage handlers, custodians, and one very pretty flight attendant. He wanted to leave, but he could not.

How we view those moments or hours or days that we are stuck, stranded, or delayed can make all the difference in the world. I was stranded, yes. But stranded in comfort and quite content to stay put. My furry friend was stuck and clinging to wet wood for life. Viktor was delayed, and he longed to leave—but made the best of each day he was forced to spend in the terminal.

Whether we are able to see it or not, God is with us in our tight spots. Are you stuck, stranded, or delayed?

> God is our refuge and strength, a very present help in trouble. Therefore we will not fear, though the earth should change and though the mountains slip into the heart of the sea; though its waters roar and foam, though the mountains quake at its swelling pride. . . . The LORD of hosts is with us; the God of Jacob is our stronghold.
>
> Psalm 46:1–3, 11

If the choice were left to us, none of us would elect to be stuck, stranded, or delayed. But sometimes we are. If that describes your situation today, surrender your rights. Submit to God's timetable. And remember that rains, floods, and even governmental red tape are not beyond his notice—or his authority.

Beautiful Interior

*M*y city has a free monthly paper that I call the "pretty people paper." It's a slick, four-color, multisectioned tabloid packed with gorgeous ads from trendy retailers I seldom recognize, much less frequent. I pick it up sometimes at the coffee shop and leave it when I'm done. It's a little like *People* magazine—hardly any copy worth remembering but lots of photos and an eye-catching cover.

The "pretty people" in their paper are photographed in bunches and posing solo at charity events, boutique openings, art and fashion shows, and private gatherings. They're well-dressed, sleek, tanned, and sometimes a little too obviously botoxed. I can't imagine any of them in Levi's or sweats—and certainly not sweating.

Every now and then I see someone I know in the pretty people paper. But mostly I see strangers. I like to look at it anyway. It's like taking a field trip to a place in your own neighborhood that you've heard about but never once visited.

Now, the pretty people paper is even thrown in my front yard. (Evidently, the coffee shop distribution was not yielding its advertisers enough readership.) One day I picked it up and placed it on the porch before taking a morning walk. And on a street I walk down at least three times a week, I passed a house I've probably passed a hundred times. I don't remember noticing the house before, but on this walk I did. And I noticed it because of the "for sale" sign out front. Under the realtor's name and phone number were these words: "I'm beautiful inside."

I looked again at the house, one of the plainest on the block. White wood. Whitewashed brick. A white front door and white shutters. Just a plain white, two-story, plantation style home—probably built in the late '30s, remodeled in the '80s or '90s, and maybe recently "botoxed" inside for the realtor to show. But evidently, it wasn't working. It wasn't pretty enough *outside*.

I remembered a recent conversation with two dear friends—women I know well and love dearly, both of whom I consider very attractive. We talked about outward appearances and how they can fool you. About our diligence to groom the "outside," because that's what the world most often judges by.

The realtor's sign said, "I'm beautiful inside," because the outside was, well, "iffy." The translation was: "I haven't got much curb appeal, but you really mustn't let that stop you. Do call, and look inside. You won't be sorry that you did."

I've been thinking about that sign. I'm thinking I'd rather live up to it than the slick images in the tabloid. I'd like to be beautiful inside. Although it's fun to glance at, I don't aspire to make the pretty people paper. I don't run in those circles—and that's okay. And while I'm not about to stop working with the exterior I've got, what I'd really like is to be unexpectedly, delightfully, utterly beautiful inside.

After all, I'd be in *such* good company.

The servant grew up before God—a scrawny seedling, a scrubby plant in a parched field. There was nothing attractive about him, nothing to cause us to take a second look. He was looked down on and passed over, a man who suffered and who knew pain firsthand. One look at him and people turned away.

Isaiah 53:2–3 Message

If people were repulsed by the "beautiful inside" Son of God, how can I be surprised by the world's emphasis on external attractiveness today? Jesus was highly esteemed by God, and he is my beautiful, beloved Savior. But part of his beauty is that he was afflicted for me and knew pain firsthand. Because he means to transform me into his image, I will joyfully receive from him all that it will take to make me truly beautiful inside.

41

School Days

*I*t had been a long time since I laced up new sneakers and headed out the front door with a sack lunch, a Big Chief tablet, a couple of sharpened pencils, and a racing heart. This time I wore sandals instead of sneakers, grabbed a cup of coffee-to-go and my Daytimer, and drove *myself* to class. I can't speak for the 128 young students I met at the inner-city private academy I visited, but here's what I learned on my first day back at school:

Ages and stages matter. Concepts that are reflexive to a five-year-old are still a mystery when you're three. Just lining up to go down the hall is fraught with challenge. Which way do you face? How close do you stand to the person in front of you? Do you stand on one leg, or both? Where do your hands go, and does the line leader (who's no bigger than you are) really know the way? Probably not. But the teacher does.

Simple rules are golden. They can get you where you need to go. Ignoring them gets you nowhere. The rules make it possible for you to hear and understand what is being taught, get along with others, and make the most of your day in class. I wrote some of them down in my notebook because, while I'm not in the classroom any longer, I *am* still learning and I think they'll help: *Be attentive. Be respectful. Be kind. Be neat. Be positive.*

A road map reassures. If you're new to any routine, knowing the way things will go (if not how they'll go) is reassuring. It's reassuring to look at the board and see that now you're on "writing," and that "breakfast" is next. That "circle" comes before "centers," and that "lunch" will follow "art." Seeing yourself in the flow of something bigger helps you to relax and enjoy the ride.

Love is the killer ingredient. I asked a teacher on this first day how long it would take him to learn all sixteen of his students' names—most of which were not easily remembered or spelled. It was third period, and he said, "By the end of the day today. I've already got most of them memorized." I don't think he had a photographic memory, although he might have. What I think is that he already *loved* them, so the learning was made easy.

Sitting at my own desk later, I watched three yellow school buses lumber down my street. I could hear kids at the school crossing four houses down, and the tweeting of the crossing guard's whistle. It was time again for school to begin, and I was sorry I'd ever let it end. I keep my pencils sharpened year-round now. I'm ready to go. Because I want to learn those lessons that my Teacher has for me, today and every day.

Show me how you work, God; school me in your ways.

Psalm 25:4 Message

Are you moving forward in your spiritual instruction? Does your understanding match your spiritual "age"? Are you being tutored by God's commands so that you may begin to walk in obedience? Do you love your lessons because you love your Teacher? Stay in school. There is still so much to learn.

Comfortably Incarcerated

*A*midst enormous media scrutiny, federal inmate number 555170–054 reported to a detention center for women in Alderson, West Virginia, known by locals and residents as "Camp Cupcake." Martha Stewart's sentence meant that Camp Cupcake would become her temporary home, far from her usual galaxy of power and ease.

It wasn't Martha's prison of choice, the newspapers noted. Our prisons seldom are. She preferred the facility in Danbury, Connecticut, for its proximity to her aging mother—but that request was denied. So Ms. Stewart came to reside in Alderson, where during her "residency" (or incarceration) she was afforded the opportunity to learn a foreign language, catch up on her reading, dabble in organic gardening, and even study religion. Oddly, that agenda might have been copied from one of the calendars that appears on the pages of the monthly magazine bearing her name. Although she could choose *what* to do, the *where* was settled in a court of law.

Comfortably incarcerated, Martha was free to select her activities and roam as far as the fences on her federal "estate," but she was not allowed to leave. Her situation has caused me to wonder how many of us are comfortably incarcerated too.

We may appear to be functioning well, or perhaps even artfully thriving, like Martha-disciples. But invisible fences of anger, or fear, or self-pity, or rage, or regret, or addiction, or abuse hold us fast in prisons not of our choosing. Our days may be filled with seemingly normal, even productive goings-on, but we know the truth—even if others can't see it. *We should be able to leave whenever we wish, but we can't. We're held fast and going nowhere.*

Martha Stewart and others like her have an undeniable advantage over ordinary, everyday prisoners. They know with some certainty the length of their sentences, and when they have served them, they are required to leave. Their comfortable incarcerations have a definite beginning and a definite ending. They are not allowed to overstay their welcome.

Some of us, on the other hand, are all but begging to be kicked out of the cages we've grown accustomed to. Prison is not our natural habitat. We don't belong in bondage, no matter how seemingly safe and tolerable our cells have become. We are sons and daughters of a great King, and our ransom has been paid in full. Isn't it time for us to open the doors we're cowering behind and walk in the freedom already won for us?

> But now that you have come to know God, or rather to be known by God, how is it that you turn back again to the weak and worthless elemental things, to which you desire to be enslaved all over again? . . . And you brethren, like Isaac, are children of promise. . . . It was for freedom that Christ set us free; therefore keep standing firm and do not be subject again to a yoke of slavery.
>
> Galatians 4:9, 28; 5:1

Sometimes it's hard to recognize a prison of our own making. Would you be brave enough to ask a friend or loved one, "Is there anything keeping me shut off from the world? Is there an unlocked cell I refuse to leave?" Jesus said the truth will set us free, and he himself claimed to be the way, the truth, and the life. One of my favorite hymns says: "He breaks the power of cancelled sin, He sets the prisoner free . . ." It seems strange that "cancelled sin" would wield any power at all, but it will always have whatever power we give it.

Conformed or Transformed?

$\mathcal{B}$ecause it was Election Day, I did something I don't normally do: I visited the seventy-year-old elementary school at the end of my block. It's the kind of facility they don't build anymore: long, high-ceilinged hallways; classroom doors with transoms, and lots of patterned tile work on the floors and walls. The school is a bright, cheerful place—but at 7:00 in the morning, it wasn't filled yet with students, only with sleepy neighbors, coffee cups in hand, inching slowly toward the library/polling place to cast their votes, then travel on to work.

It took a while for the line to begin moving, so I perused artwork as I waited. Lockers were brightly decorated with students' names, and posters espousing values like "caring" and "tolerance" and "kindness" and "cooperation" competed for wall space with class projects of every imaginable kind.

My favorite stuff in the hallway gallery was done by Ms. Sanders's class. It seems they had been studying "biomes" (where was *I* in elementary school?) and how animals adapt themselves to their environment. Their assignment apparently was to create new animals based on a particular biome's characteristics and describe their invented animal and his suitability to it.

The creatures these kids created were nothing short of delightful. There was the many-legged "octocrab," suited to a marine biome but fast-moving over sand—and the "tundra-marsupialite" outfitted for high altitude living. The "squeazle" was a lean desert rat that absorbed water like a sponge, and the fur-finned "polar bunny" resided (and swam) in arctic climes. As wonderful as their drawings were, the children's descriptions of their made-up animals' traits were even better. They'd really thought this stuff through. They were creating animals that were über-suited to their living places.

As I examined their work, I thought about how we humans adapt to *our* surroundings. How we play up or down certain aspects of our personalities in order to survive or thrive—and how we sometimes behave differently depending on who's watching. I thought about softhearted people who act tough to cover up their hurt, and about frightened people who boast or bully to mask their fear. I thought of people who eat or starve to be in control, and of those who withhold the very thing they're aching to receive because they don't believe they'll ever have enough.

There are many differences between us and the animals, between their "biomes" and our homes and workplaces and houses of worship. But one telling difference is this: our ability to survive and thrive is not dependent on conforming—it's dependent on being *transformed.* We won't improve with "outer" adaptations. We'll get better and stronger only with inner regeneration. Because we're not made to be conformed from the outside in. We're created to be transformed from the inside out.

> Take your everyday, ordinary life—your sleeping, eating, going-to-work, and walking-around life—and place it before God as an offering . . . Don't become so well-adjusted to your culture that you fit into it without even thinking. Instead, fix your attention on God. You'll be changed from the inside out.
>
> Romans 12:1–2 Message

I'm guilty of overediting. I frequently edit myself according to the context of my surroundings—choosing my words and the face I show the world based on who or what happens to be nearby. And it's exhausting work. What I should be doing instead is allowing the Author of my story to edit my heart, my thoughts, and my desires, based on the unchanging and beautiful standard of his own perfect nature. But how things "should" be is not always how they are.

Fridays at Avalon

*E*very Friday between 7 and 7:30 a.m., I meet my dad for breakfast at a drugstore / café called The Avalon Diner. Unless one of us is out of town or under the weather, it's a standing deal. We only call if we *can't* make it . . . not to be sure the other one is coming.

We haven't always met at the Avalon. For a while we convened at a diner closer to my old apartment, then at a trendier place near my former office that Dad endured but never really liked. The location has shifted over the years, but the routine hasn't. It's become something comfortable that I can count on.

I can't remember when we started the Friday breakfast thing—or when it became a standing appointment on my calendar. I feel safe in saying it's been at least fifteen years . . . maybe even longer. For the last few years, when she can crawl out of bed that early, my oldest niece has taken to joining us. She attends a university barely a mile from our spot—and like any other college student, appreciates a meal she doesn't have to pay for. (I like to think our company compels her occasionally too.)

At the Avalon, the coffee is plentiful and hot. Cassie usually takes care of our table . . . a job her embroidered apron says she has held since the year I started third grade. When Cassie's out, it's Sarah, another longtime employee. On the rare occasions when I go there alone, one or the other of them will ask, "Where's Mac?" They've gotten used to our routine as well.

48

I guess by now we've had hundreds upon hundreds of Friday morning breakfasts. I've gotten business advice, heard stories about my dad's Navy years and relatives I barely remember . . . talked politics and faith and finances. We've agreed and disagreed, both agreeably and (rarely) disagreeably. I can't honestly recall the details of many of those conversations, but I do remember their tenor. It's easy and familiar, like the green vinyl booth we slide into, right-hand side, closest to the kitchen. And I can count on one hand the mornings I've beat him there.

I like coming up the sidewalk, looking in the glass front of the Avalon, and seeing the top of Dad's head (grayer and with less hair than when we started this thing) bent over the paper, or his daily to-do list. I like that someone's waiting there for me without me having to ask or arrange it. And I like how his presence reminds me of the simple goodness of my *other* Father's faithfulness . . . the One who always waits for me.

> Know therefore that the LORD your God, He is God, the faithful God, who keeps His covenant and His lovingkindness to a thousandth generation with those who love Him and keep His commandments.
>
> Deuteronomy 7:9

There's no set agenda at Avalon. We just show up. I sometimes imagine that God wants me to have a very organized, noble agenda in mind when I meet with him, but maybe, like Dad, he's just always glad to see me arrive. A day will come when neither Dad nor I will be at Avalon. But thankfully, a day will never come when I will not be in my heavenly Father's presence. He's promised, and I believe him.

My Beautiful Desert

"I feel so untethered and ungrounded," I told a trusted friend. "None of the things I've counted on seem certain anymore. The only thing I'm still sure of is God." He didn't shrink back at my words or fall away in a dead faint. My confession didn't rock his world one bit. He didn't offer easy platitudes, either, or point me to his favorite Scripture. He just nodded knowingly and said, "That's good enough." And he was right.

This isn't exactly a season of plenty. My barns aren't full and I'm in no way thinking of building new ones. My surest comforts aren't so comforting anymore, and my sweetest dreams seem almost silly when I name them, so I don't. But even in this desert, even in this odd and awful wilderness, my God keeps coming at me, relentless in his love. He just keeps turning up.

In an unexpected bouquet of tulips and gerbera daisies left on my doorstep with a handmade card. In a friend's well-timed email, brimming with love. In the first pink rose on the well-pruned hedge out back, defiant in its solitude and daring any future frost to set spring back, even for an hour. In a long-distance prayer, prayed out loud for me on the telephone while I held the receiver and wept. In a plate of fish tacos shared in the sweet presence of a true and faithful friend. In the exquisite sliver of moon that hung so low in the sky last night that I almost reached for it.

How can I be sure it's him? Who else makes the desert bloom? Who causes rivers to run in dry places and the wilderness to bear fruit? Exactly.

I'm not sure about tomorrow. I'm not even sure about this afternoon. I'm not sure that the check is in the mail, or the cavalry is coming, or that dreams will come true or happily-ever-after is around the bend.

What I *am* sure of is this: God can make joy out of almost nothing. "Joy," said Stanley Hauerwas, "is the disposition that comes from the realization that we can trust in surprises to sustain our lives." He still surprises me. I think he always will.

> Indeed, the LORD will comfort Zion; He will comfort all her waste places. And her wilderness He will make like Eden, and her desert like the garden of the LORD; joy and gladness will be found in her, thanksgiving and the sound of a melody.
>
> Isaiah 51:3

I love that phrase, "make . . . her desert like the garden of the LORD." Only God can do that. Only he can make what looks bleak, barren, and hopeless into something fresh and green and growing. Are you counting on God to surprise you—or are you bemoaning your present desert? Open your heart wider to see its stark beauty . . . and trust that living water is indeed making all things new.

Six A.M. Saxophone

A passionate person lives three blocks east of me and two blocks south. We've never met; I don't know his or her age or occupation or life circumstances. I do know that he (or she) is passionate enough about mastering the saxophone to practice it very early in the morning. (And I'll bet his more immediate neighbors know it too.)

How do I know? Because as I've walked in the early light, just before sunrise, I've heard the notes that come from behind the door of a certain house on a certain street—and I've heard them more than once. The first time it took a while to zero in on their source, but far less time to determine that the music wasn't coming from a CD player or radio. It simply wasn't that polished. This six a.m. saxophone player starts and stops, stumbles, then picks up momentum, and moves from long, shaky notes to rolling riffs and back without much seeming direction. Once I pinpointed where the music came from, it sounded like so much fun that I slowed down to listen.

I'm not sure what sort of person plays the saxophone behind his door at six a.m., but I *am* sure it's not a professional musician. Maybe it's a doctor or lawyer or teacher or salesman who showers when his mini-concert is ended and dresses for the day at his real job. And all the while, at that real job, underneath a lab coat or wrinkled shirt or uniform, the heart of a jazz man beats.

Most mornings, I start my day with a walk, then a shower, and then a good cup of coffee slowly sipped while I read. Sometimes I linger over the poetry of the Psalms, or the drama of Acts, or the mysterious images of Leviticus or Revelation. Sometimes I go straight for the God-in-the-flesh comfort of Matthew, Mark, Luke, or John. I savor bits and pieces of God's story at six a.m., and taken in that way they don't make a complete, cohesive whole. But every line of it is beautiful, and all of it is true. And I'm passionate about lingering over each and every word until I get it right.

Maybe when I go out for the day I still have the look of someone who's tasted the extraordinary for breakfast. I hope I do. I hope I look like a woman with a secret passion, who'd be willing to spill the beans about it if you gave her half a chance. Because, like my neighbor down the way who's playing his riffs at dawn, I'm a little crazy about something that's not my real job—and I'm not too terribly worried about who knows.

But if I say, "I will not remember Him or speak anymore in His name," then in my heart it becomes like a burning fire shut up in my bones; and I am weary of holding it in, and I cannot endure it.

Jeremiah 20:9

We can—and do—make time for what we love most. It's the nature of love to crowd lesser things out and to seek its own expression and nurture. Is your love for God something you'd practice at six a.m. if that were the best time to ensure you'd be focused and uninterrupted? What does your daily routine say about your own passions? Can those around you tell with certainty what you love?

Ant Street Expectations

I'd wrapped up a couple of large work projects and decided that a few days away from the phone, computer, and doorbell were just what I needed. I didn't want to fly, or drive for hours, either—so I booked a room at a small bed and breakfast barely an hour from home and took off. The innkeeper met me at the door the afternoon I arrived, and handed me a key on an old brass ring. She carried my bag up a worn and creaky staircase to a beautiful second-floor parlor and then to my many-windowed room—on a corner at the back of the old building, away from any hustle and bustle or street noise.

I thought it was perfect . . . for a while.

Then I reviewed the fire escape plan and saw that the room I was in was the inn's smallest by far. I looked around me at the exposed brick and slate-colored walls, and they seemed to close in. In the morning I went downstairs for breakfast (as in bed *and* breakfast) and found one grumpy man reading the only *Houston Chronicle* in sight. "Were you looking for something?" he asked, as if my presence were an intrusion. I eyed his paper then peeked into the dark and empty dining room. "Coffee?" I asked—thinking he'd surely offer more.

He rather grudgingly put down the paper I was hoping to read myself and said he'd get me some. No mention was made of breakfast. He poured me a Styrofoam go-cup and asked if I needed a lid too. "If it wouldn't be too much trouble," I said. Apparently it wasn't.

When I returned to the inn at nearly 2 p.m., I opened the door to my room and found my bed still unmade. I was becoming less and less enamored with Ant Street. Never mind that I make my bed every day at home. Here, I expected something more. Here, I expected that someone else would do it for me. Soon I began to notice small deficiencies I had not recognized before: the tiny coffeemaker in my room was missing the filter basket, making it impossible to use. The advertised seventh tall window was right across from the shower door, making it (to my mind anyway) rather a moot point, except to an exhibitionist. Wouldn't it have been more truthful to say *six* tall windows?

My expectations were taking a pounding in this place. I had wanted to be pampered, and instead I felt ignored.

The final morning of my stay I ventured downstairs even earlier, thinking perhaps I'd find the dining room open and the reception kinder. Not a soul in sight. So I loaded my bags into the car, picked up the newspaper from the sidewalk outside and placed it on the counter, along with my key. I'd planned some rather unkind words for whoever might have asked me, "How was your stay with us?" Thankfully for them, no one did.

As I drove home I realized that my satisfaction with my two days off was based wholly on unmet expectations, even though parts of the time were lovely. A thunderstorm had rumbled through late at night and made the small/ tall room seem cozy and warm. I'd watched two workers string Christmas lights on the courthouse gazebo, and a waitress at the diner across the street from the B&B called me "darlin'" when she poured my coffee. The leaves on the trees just off the back balcony had rustled in the wind like applause when I finished writing my Christmas poem, and the train whistles blew so long and low they made my heart ache to hear them.

I got far less than I expected from my time at Ant Street and much more than I deserved. God is so good that way.

And they forgot His deeds, and His miracles that He had shown them.

Psalm 78:11

My expectations are the source of my dissatisfaction, oh, say, nine times out of ten. If I can let go of them, I'm better able to enjoy what comes to me from the gracious hand of God. When I cling to them, I almost always feel cheated or disappointed—and worse—overlook what is already mine, which is often better for me than any of the items on my "want" list.

Right Track, Wrong Train

A while back I found myself a little lost in Chicago. Not a lot lost, just a little. I stood on the "El" platform at Roosevelt and waited for the commuter train that would carry me to Midway, then a flight home. I'd come into town on the "El" orange line and was going back the same way. It was chilly out—warm for November by Chicago standards but cold for a Gulf Coast girl—and windy. So when a southbound train rumbled up to the platform and people began lining up to board, I lined up with them. And got on.

At first, as we began heading due south, everything looked familiar. The same "fringe" of the Chicago loop, and the same impossibly tight squeezes past apartment buildings whose windows seemed close enough to touch. (How *do* those people sleep at night?) Then we passed U.S. Cellular Field, where the White Sox play, and I didn't recall seeing it before. I glanced up and noticed that the route map inside the car was green—not orange. I looked around me and saw no one with luggage. At all. And when I asked the woman next to me if this was the train to Midway, she said "Oh, no, honey. That's the orange. You got to get off."

So, at the next stop, I did. Only the next stop bore a strong resemblance to a bombed-out alley, where I had to walk down a rickety flight of stairs, across a narrow street, and into another station to access the *northbound* side of the same platform. I needed to go back the way I came and begin again. I had been at the right station and on the right track. But I boarded the wrong train, which became evident enough in time.

Do you ever find yourself in such a spot? You imagined you were doing everything right, but somehow you ended up in a place you never planned to be. And the only comfort in such a place is that you might be able to return to where you first erred and try again.

I'm on the right track as far as God is concerned. My faith rests in Christ, and it rests solidly. But sometimes I get a little turned around. Mixed up. Confused. I know who I am following—but I'm not always sure I've heard him correctly. George MacDonald said it this way in his *Diary of an Old Soul*:

56

I know what Thou will'st—only keep me sure
That Thou art willing: call to me now and then.
So, ceasing to enjoy, I shall endure
With perfect patience—willing beyond my ken,
Beyond my love, beyond my thinking scope;
Willing to be because thy will is pure;
Willing thy will beyond all bounds of hope.[3]

Is this way the right way? I believe it is. I believe I've heard your voice, Father . . . but the landscape changes so quickly. I could be on the right track, but riding the wrong train. Just call to me now and then, and I'll go willingly. I really *do* want to get it right. I really *do* mean to follow you.

The path of the righteous is level; O upright One, you make the way of the righteous smooth. Yes, LORD, walking in the way of your laws, we wait for you; your name and renown are the desire of our hearts.

Isaiah 26:7–8 NIV

If I hadn't realized when I did that I was on the wrong train, I might have ended up in a far scarier place than the one where I did finally disembark. If I'd been very, very sure of my "rightness," I probably would have missed my flight altogether. It's good to check my spiritual whereabouts now and then too, and ask, "Is this it, God? Is this the way you mean for me to go? I want to be sure I am following where you lead."

Part 2

Ordinary People

Ten Fingers and Ten Toes

For years she was "the dream." For months, she was "the bump." Ultrasonic pictures of her temporary home revealed her gender, and then she had a name. Her presence was quite obvious. Her mother could feel her move. But even so, she didn't seem so real. Not yet.

Yesterday all of that changed. Yesterday she made her appearance into a brand-new world: new to her because she'd never seen a bit of it before. New to all of us because she's in it.

I'm a daughter, a sister, a friend, a cousin, an aunt, a niece ... but not a mom. So I'd never before seen a tiny, carefully knit and lovingly carried newborn make the jarring break from one world to another, take her first pure breaths of air and meet the ones who—together with God—made her. But yesterday I did.

Yesterday I saw a kind of "special delivery" I may never see again. This one has ten tiny fingers and ten tiny toes. She came slipping and gasping and crying into a cold, brightly lit room where she was the center of everything— and everyone there was glad to see her. Let me be the first to say she didn't look a *thing* like her pictures. They didn't do her justice at all. There's just no comparing a flat gray, fuzzy image to six squirming, bleating pounds or so of miracle. None.

Safely detached from the only comfort she'd ever known, she was held high for all to see, then whisked off to an adjoining room where she underwent a regimen that, to me at least, seemed a little rough in light of all she'd just endured. She was vigorously wiped, rubbed, and turned from side to side. Pulled, prodded, and poked. The soles of her little feet were thumped to make her breathe and cry more deeply—then inked and pressed onto the paper that declared her birth, as if she were some tiny felon.

I know it's obvious, but I still can't help thinking: *this is how we all got here.* This rough, wild entrance into another reality is one thing we all share. Once we lived in the safest place imaginable, and now we're all out in the bright light of day, trying to make the best of a world that is unpredictable and sometimes cruel, but shot through with wonder just the same. And here's the other thing we share: we have another world, a wilder, brighter, richer, deeper one than this awaiting us. What lies beyond bears no more resemblance to what we have seen so far than this baby's "tummy pictures" did to her stunningly brilliant appearing.

Welcome to our world, sweet girl. Jesus loves you, even now. He brought you here with us . . . and with us, he is sure to bring you just as safely home.

> You know me inside and out, you know every bone in my body; you know exactly how I was made, bit by bit, how I was sculpted from nothing into something. Like an open book, you watched me grow from conception to birth; all the stages of my life were spread out before you, the days of my life all prepared before I'd even lived one day.
>
> Psalm 139:14–16 Message

Seeing a baby being born places Jesus's words to Nicodemus ("You must be born again") in a whole new light. To be born is to move from one reality to another. To be detached from one "support system" and be thrust into a new one. To leave all that you've ever known for something you've never seen. What a radical idea! What a brilliant reality!

Who Is My Neighbor?

I can call most of my neighbors—at least the nearest ones—by name. But every now and then I wonder if I would readily ask any of them for help, should I need it—or just how willing I would be to offer help to them. We know each others' names—but does that make us neighbors?

Of course, I'm not the first person that's wondered about the neighbors. The gospel of Luke says "a certain lawyer" who wanted to put Jesus to the test asked him what he should do to inherit eternal life. Jesus asked him what was written in the law (I can almost see the legal expert rubbing his palms together at *this* juicy question!), and he answered, "You shall love the Lord your God with all your heart, and with all your soul, and with all your strength, and with all your mind; and your neighbor as yourself" (Luke 10:27).

Jesus told him he had answered correctly. But the man wasn't nearly done "lawyering," so he posed a follow-up: "And who is my neighbor?" Then Jesus told a story about a crime victim and his unlikely rescuer. Suffice it to say the definition of "neighbor" was neatly expanded.

Last week I met a new neighbor (three, really.) On the way to an early evening meeting I experienced a pretty spectacular blowout on my right rear tire. Luckily I was only two blocks from home when it happened, so I pulled over to the curb on a residential street, locked my car, and walked back to the house, trying to figure out whom I could call to change a tire at the close of a business day.

As providence would have it, an elder from my church had planned to drop off a packet of materials at my door while I was out—and when he arrived with the package, I was in! I remembered a nearby service station that had changed a flat for me before but could not recall the name.

Could he drive by it when he left and call me with the information? He would be glad to, he said.

But he didn't stop there. A few minutes later this brand-new neighbor was at my door with another neighbor: a fellow who worked at the station and who was ready (at the close of business) to change my tire. "New neighbor one" took "new neighbor two" and me to my stranded car, where neighbor two and I began the "finding the spare and tools" process. Only this kind fellow's English wasn't too good, so when we found the owner's manual instructions, he looked at the pictures while I read the words out loud. A short cell phone call (in another language) brought another of his co-workers. Now there were three of us, and in short order, the tire was changed—but not before their place of business had closed. Could I pay them cash there? No, they both said, come by the station tomorrow, and we will have your tire fixed and ready for you. You can pay us then.

The next day I did stop in—and all was ready, as promised. As I paid, new neighbor two cheerfully handed me a business card for the station. "Call us whenever you need help," he said. Then he carefully printed his name on the card: "Nedal." He handed it to me, smiled, and (I swear) said these words to me: "I am your neighbor." And he was.

> But a Samaritan, who was on a journey, came upon him; and when he saw him, he felt compassion.
>
> Luke 10:33

Nedal didn't help me because he was my neighbor. He was my neighbor because he went out of his way to help me. Who is your neighbor? Whose neighbor are you?

Con Affetto, Please

The Sybarite Quintet was born in 1997 when a group of five young string players decided to perform chamber music on an Aspen, Colorado, street corner. I heard them years later in that same town when, with my eighteen-year-old niece, we walked to Paradise Bakery for a smoothie and stumbled onto a musical serendipity.

Drinks in hand, we settled on a bench on the small patio outside the bakery and watched as five musicians unpacked and tuned their instruments. All were young but seemed quite comfortable with the crowd that had begun to press in as they prepared. Couples with children clutching ice-cream cones. An elderly gentleman in neatly pressed khakis. Two guys in jogging wear, stopping their run to listen. A gaggle of Dallasites in pastel polo shirts, laughing loudly at some shared joke. A couple next to us on the bench with a sleeping Sheltie in their laps. It seemed as if many who gathered had come just for this. Not us. We were simply in the right place at the right time.

Tuned up and ready, the double bass player announced the first piece, and the ensemble—double bass, two violins, cello, and viola—launched into an hour and a half of glorious music. We heard Stravinsky, Vivaldi, and Brahms. Rogers and Hammerstein and Led Zeppelin. If I had closed my eyes the music would have been just as beautiful, but after a very short time of people watching, I couldn't take my eyes off the young woman playing violin.

I'm not sure she was a "regular" member of the group. (I did some Internet research on them when we got home and couldn't find her picture or her name.) Maybe she was a musical angel—or more likely, a visiting student at the local music festival. Whatever she was, she was mesmerizing. I'm not a very sophisticated connoisseur of classical music, but I've never seen a violinist play that small instrument with her whole *body*.

Every muscle, every sinew, every nerve seemed connected to the wrist that held her bow, and to her neck, arched over her instrument. It seemed as if each note resonated in her, just below her skin—and was racing to emerge through her hands, her fingers, and into the night air. I was sitting slightly to the side of her, and so I rarely caught a glimpse of her face. But I was close enough to see her pour herself, *con affetto*, into every line and phrase.

Finally, the sun dipped below the horizon, and the air began to chill. The empty instrument case on the sidewalk was filled with bills of all denominations, and the musicians bid us good night. Victoria and I walked to a nearby restaurant and had a light dinner. But I kept thinking about this woman who played with such emotion, such passion—and pondering this question: what if I *lived* like she played? Full of energy, completely engaged, captured head to toe with the delight of doing what I was made for?

She had found that place where her joy and the world's hunger met—even just for a little while. And I was blessed.

> You . . . have clothed me with gladness, that my glory may sing your praise and not be silent. O LORD my God, I will give thanks to you forever!
>
> Psalm 30:11–12 ESV

Are you playing your part with passion? Have you discovered the sweet spot where your great love and the world's great hunger meet?

A Hero in the Wings

$\mathcal{B}$y the time Jason McElwain was a senior in high school, he had done two things I've never done and certainly never will: scored twenty points in four minutes in a varsity basketball game and sit on Oprah Winfrey's couch to talk about it.

Jason wasn't really a player on the varsity team to begin with. He has autism and was accustomed to being (and happy to be) on the sidelines, chasing stray balls, gathering up towels, and clapping and encouraging the "real" players at every opportunity. As a reward for his dedication, his coach let him suit up for his very last home game—and to everyone's shock and surprise, he called Jason to the floor with four minutes left in the game.[1]

Then Jason did something I would never have dared to do. He shot the ball! He didn't just stand by, delighted to let the others play around him. When he got in the game, he got in the game. His first shot was an air ball attempt. (Again, I would have quit there, in mortification.) Jason didn't. He shot again. Another miss. Then on his third attempt, Jason connected on a nothing-but-net three-pointer. The crowd went wild.

In the final minutes of a game he never expected to play, Jason sank *five more* three-point shots. His last one ripped the net as the final buzzer went off, and Jason's "new" teammates carried their hero out on their shoulders. The gymnasium erupted in cheering, foot-stomping mayhem. His parents and his coach wept. When I saw the whole thing on video, I did too.

Jason's dad said that one of the greatest moments of his life was "watching the kids start cheering, and chanting [Jason's] name."

This would be a great story—an incredibly great story—even if I didn't believe what I believe. But because I believe in another hero in the wings, I love Jason's story even more.

Seven hundred or so years before his appearing, the prophet Isaiah predicted the coming of another unlikely hero: a Savior who would deliver his people from their own sin and guilt. He would be a king, but he wouldn't look like a king. He would be great, but his greatness would be mostly under wraps. Just like Jason's.

When this king did appear, he made his entrance in a very humble way. He grew up in a small town. His parents were small-town people. He didn't do much to distinguish himself until he was thirty, and when he claimed to be the Messiah, most people didn't buy it. But he was a hero who waited patiently in the wings.

When his moment came, he seized it. And although it hasn't happened yet, one day everyone will see him for who he really is, so "that at the name of Jesus every knee should bow, in heaven and on earth and under the earth, and every tongue confess that Jesus Christ is Lord" (Phil. 2:10–11 NIV), and his Father will no doubt delight in the sound of them calling his name.

> He grew up . . . like a young plant,
>   and like a root out of dry ground;
> he had no form or majesty that we should look
>   at him,
>   and no beauty that we should desire him.
> He was despised and rejected by men;
>   . . . and we esteemed him not.
>
> Isaiah 53:2–3

Jesus was a surprise to those who were alive at his first coming. He was not the hero they expected. But unlikely heroes are often the very best kind.

The Kindness of Strangers

*L*ike a lot of other Texans, I ran from what was supposed to be a catastrophic hurricane headed straight for the Gulf Coast and closing in fast. When multiple meteorologists and elected officials took to the airwaves to warn us that a category five storm was bearing down, nearly 2.5 million of us took their advice and evacuated.

If I had known when I left my home that I was about to spend eighteen hours in a barely moving car, two-thirds of that time without air-conditioning, on a day that temperatures reached 100°—I can assure you I would have reconsidered. I don't remember when I have been more exhausted, frightened, or lonely.

But I was not alone. Not by a long shot.

Throughout the day and night, I spoke with family and friends by cell phone. Signals were hard to come by, but when I needed to get through, I could. And when I needed encouragement most, someone got through to me. When it looked as if I would run out of gas before I reached my destination, I thought of God providing oil for lamps and bread for multitudes, and I asked him for fossil fuel. I was the twenty-fifth car in line at the only gas station I'd seen for miles, and I filled my tank.

I struck up a conversation with a man and his wife in front of me, who'd left Houston six hours after I had. He looked in my car, saw my dog, and asked if I was traveling alone. I said I was. He asked where I was going, and I told him my hoped-for destination. His was along the same road, some fifty miles closer. We wished each other well and drove off as the sun was setting. In the dead of dark, nearly two hours later, he pulled up next to me and waved as he made his turn. He had followed me the entire way.

The friend I was planning to stay with lived another three hours (normal driving time) away, and when it grew very late, she called her former college roommate in a town closer to me and asked if I could stay the night there. This dear woman and her husband graciously said yes and took me in—at 11:30 at night, with my dog in tow.

They not only took me in, they made me feel at home. And they prepared a place for me that was lovely and peaceful and cool. I don't remember a shower ever feeling so good, or a bed so soft.

The next day, I made my way to my intended destination and fell into the arms of a friend. But I had never been out of the arms of my Father. He really does know *everyone* — and he led me safely home.

"Then the king will say to those on his right: 'Come, you who have won my Father's blessing! Take your inheritance—the kingdom reserved for you since the foundation of the world! For I was hungry and you gave me food. I was thirsty and you gave me a drink. I was lonely, and you made me welcome.'"

Matthew 25:34–35 Phillips

Have you experienced the kindness of strangers? Have you extended that same kindness to those who are strangers to you? I was a stranger at Jack and Freda's, and they opened their doors to me as if they'd known me for ages. Their hospitality made me feel at home, even though we'd just met. How great is it that God has family everywhere?

The Balcony Dancer

*O*ut of the fifth-floor window of a downtown Denver hotel room, something in motion caught my eye. I was only vaguely aware of it before I looked, the way you're aware of an insect buzzing nearby: you sense it, but unless it lingers or comes closer, you don't turn in its direction. The peripheral distraction continued, though, so I set down my coffee cup, laid aside the newspaper, and focused my eyes on *it*, instead of on the day's headlines.

"It" was someone on the balcony of a nearby building—across the street and just slightly below me. At first I thought the person was a child waving his arms wildly at someone just inside the glass . . . but a closer look revealed that it wasn't a child at all. It was a child-sized woman doing what must have been her morning workout, dancing with all the verve and energy of an NBA cheerleader—skipping and leaping from one side of the balcony to the other in fast time and flinging her arms up and out as she went.

She moved to a beat that I couldn't hear, and she danced with the passion of someone leading a whole class of dancers behind her. Only she was utterly and completely alone on the balcony, with nothing but the brick and glass of other buildings around her. Once I realized what she was doing, I couldn't stop watching . . . waiting to see if she would eventually tire and bend over in spent exhaustion. But she didn't—not for a long time.

She danced and danced and danced. It seemed as if she was inviting the whole city to dance with her. And if there was no music in her ears from tiny earphones I couldn't see, there was music inside her somewhere. Music itching to travel through her oxygenated muscles, then off into the wind.

I wasn't so much curious about her routine, though. I was curious about her motivation. What compelled this woman to dance on the balcony before 7 a.m.? What thought or note or feeling caused her to dance with such enthusiastic abandon? Did she do it every day? (She certainly gave the impression that she *could*.)

When she did finally stop, I went back to my coffee, but instead of picking up the newspaper again, I considered what I'd seen . . . and this is what I thought: when the joy in me is so strong and pure and true that it comes out no matter where I am, the world will notice. When I express that joy with abandon, and with no thought to whether or not I have an audience, an audience (however small) will find me. And if I don't occasionally fling my arms out in praise, or leap, or cry out, or plead with my world to notice God's glory . . . someone else on some other balcony *will*. He'll get his glory. It belongs to him. The question is, will I get in on the dance?

> As soon as He was approaching, near the descent of the Mount of Olives, the whole crowd of the disciples began to praise God joyfully with a loud voice for all the miracles which they had seen, shouting: "Blessed is the King who comes in the name of the Lord; peace in heaven and glory in the highest!" Some of the Pharisees in the crowd said to Him, "Teacher, rebuke Your disciples." But Jesus answered, "I tell you, if these become silent, the stones will cry out!"
>
> Luke 19:37–40

Some urges are so strong they cannot be shamed or stifled—they simply must be expressed. Let my faith be one of these!

Spending It All

*S*everal years ago my best friend and I wandered through a palazzo in Florence, Italy, killing an hour or so before our return flight home. We'd been in Italy for nearly a week and were feeling pretty confident we could navigate its peculiar traffic, monetary, and communication mazes with some measure of ease. Not planning to return to the country anytime soon, we decided it would be a good thing to spend every lira in our pockets and headed for the nearest gelato stand to do so.

Using a combination of gestures and words, we ordered—we thought—two one-scoop cones of gelato, saying something ridiculous like "due 'big drum.'" What we got was two two-scoop cones for twice the price we'd planned. Having already licked said cones of gelato before we realized our error, we were overdrawn. We emptied the contents of our purses and pockets and still came up short. The ice-cream vendor looked at us like the idiot Americans we were and waved us out of his store. We still laugh about it today.

I was recently reminded of our "due 'big drum'" spend-it-all spree when I attended a Bible conference to hear a noted teacher. "Prof," as he's affectionately called, is surely well into his seventies. Cancer has claimed his right eye, and he wears a black eye patch now, in jarring contrast to his softly aging face. His gait was a little tentative, and his hands sometimes trembled when he gestured with them—which he did quite often. His body was clearly wearing out—but when he started speaking, he was ageless. No, he was *young*.

His voice was full of delightful inflection, and his good eye twinkled. He had fully engaged the room of mostly elderly men and women in a minute or less. He challenged those of us in his assembled classroom to live intentionally for Christ in a dying world—and he did it with passion, clarity, and power. And as he did, I thought: *he's spending it all.* He's spending every last bit of himself doing the thing he was made to do, to the glory of the One who made him. He's not worried about coming up short—he's leaving the accounting to someone else. *This man means to go out empty.*

Some of us are "savers" and some are "spenders." After watching "Prof" teach for a handful of hours, I was more sure than ever that I want to be a spender. "Right now" is a slice of time so thin it can barely be measured—but we live like this world is everything we've got—saving now to spend tomorrow, or the day after that, or the day after that. Instead, I should be about spending every last bit of what I have—energy, time, talent, passion—before it's time to go. I won't be here again. My body will age and slow and falter too, but it's not the best of what I have to offer. I'm made for spending from the inside, and the heart held by Jesus is always young.

> Therefore, my beloved brethren, be steadfast, immovable, always abounding in the work of the Lord, knowing that your toil is not in vain in the Lord.
>
> 1 Corinthians 15:58

What are you saving for? There's a peculiar glory in spending all you have for what cannot be bought at any price. Happy is the one who offers his or her treasure—all of it—with joy.

Tsunami Baby

$\mathcal{N}$ot even two months after one of the worst natural disasters in history, news of the devastation of the Indian Ocean tsunami was relegated to the inside pages of the newspaper—or the last sound bite on the nightly news. It wasn't the lead story for long. Apparently the public has a saturation point as to how much horrific detail can be absorbed.

But one story from the horrific disaster lingered longer than any other.

"Baby 81," a four-month-old Sri Lankan infant swept from his mother's arms, was finally identified, and when he was—it was news. He was pulled alive from a heap of mud, debris, and corpses, and was the eighty-first patient admitted to a small hospital in the coastal town of Kalmunai. Nine couples quickly claimed the child was theirs—and for eight weeks, officials sought to determine who "Baby 81's" parents really were.

This week they did. "Baby 81" belongs to Jenita and Murugupillai Jeyarajah—the couple who insisted from the very beginning that he was their son, Abilass. DNA tests confirmed it; the Jeyarajahs were the only couple who submitted to the testing. They knew beyond certainty that he was theirs.

I don't have children, but I can't fathom that a mother and a father would not know their own child beyond a shadow of a doubt. I can only imagine the unbearable grief at their own losses that must have made the other parents claim the surviving tsunami baby. That they would hurt enough to do so is unspeakably sad to me.

The tsunami that swept Abilass from the protective arms of his mother killed hundreds of thousands of people, orphaned children, and decimated families, homes, and towns in nearly a dozen nations. Records that might identify both victims and survivors were lost. But in his very body the little tsunami baby bore the truth about his parentage. And in the end, he could not be separated from the ones to whom he belonged.

There may come a day when any relatives or witnesses who could confirm my true identity are gone. When church records have crumbled to dust. When I can't even remember my own name. But the truth of who I am has been secured by the Holy Spirit who resides in me—and he will testify as surely as any molecular evidence that I belong to God. Like the tsunami baby, the invisible will prove what can no longer be verified . . . and there is no force large enough to separate me from the One in whose family I will permanently reside.

> The Spirit Himself testifies with our spirit that we are children of God . . . For I am convinced that neither death, nor life, nor angels, nor principalities, nor things present, nor things to come, nor powers, nor height, nor depth, nor any other created thing, will be able to separate us from the love of God, which is in Christ Jesus our Lord.
>
> Romans 8:16, 38–39

I cannot be lost. I simply cannot. I bear in my Spirit the familial mark of heredity that identifies me as a child of God. My name is written in his Book of Life. My soul is knit to his. I belong to him forever, and nothing can separate me from his love.

Sweet Sixty-five

*K*ing Solomon said, "Remember also your Creator in the days of your youth, before the evil days come and the years draw near when you will say, 'I have no delight in them'" (Eccles. 12:1). He obviously wasn't thrilled with the prospect of aging.

King Solomon never met my friend Peggy.

I recently attended a surprise luncheon celebrating her birthday. Thirty-plus friends had gathered in a lovely dining room to honor Peggy, who was turning sixty-five. (Peggy is also very likely to read this book, so, my dear friend, please forgive me for telling your age to so many strangers.)

Most of us there that day did not know one another. We knew Peggy. Some had known her for a very long time—one of the ladies at my table was a friend way back in grade school. Others cheered on her Hillsboro High School cheering squad—and had the pictures to prove it! Some were college sorority sisters, others had children who grew up with her boys, and still others like me came to know her later in life. We were, with a few exceptions, strangers to one another who became fast friends over lunch, celebrating our great good luck in being part of the circle of warmth and wisdom and laughter that surrounds the "Divine Miss N."

Throughout the luncheon lots of hugs were exchanged. Wickedly funny stories were told. An original poem about the birthday girl was recited, and its payoff line, which caused Peggy to dance with delight, was *"lightly* breaded . . . and *deeply* fried." Caution was tossed to the wind and calories were consumed with abandon. And as I watched my friend move from table to table and celebrant to celebrant, I thought, *I'm done wishing for sweet sixteen to come again. I'm aiming for sweet sixty-five.*

For the sweet sixty-five that comes from having invested in the lives of others, cheered them on, and shouldered their burdens. For the joy that comes from spending, not from hoarding—and the resiliency and thankfulness that surviving heartbreak yields. I'm aiming for wisdom and grace and beauty and peace, because my friend made sixty-five look so very sweet.

Peggy lives modestly in a smallish house in a smallish town, with a smallish garden growing out back. She drives a smallish car and worships at a smallish church. But she has not lived a smallish life. She says she's retiring . . . but I don't buy it. She's watching to see what brand-new chapter her God will unfold, and she's ready to follow him there.

As I hugged her at the party's end, I told Peggy the truest thing I knew: that she was a very, very rich woman. What I didn't tell her was this: I want to be like her when *I'm* sixty-five.

> I have inherited Your testimonies forever, for they are the joy of my heart. I have inclined my heart to perform Your statutes forever, even to the end.
>
> Psalm 119:111–12

Nothing testifies of the life that Jesus gives like joy in growing old. When someone two decades or more your senior can make you jealous for the candles on her cake—well, that's something. Maybe every day with Jesus really is sweeter, after all.

Miss Laura's Mail

About twice a month, I get a piece of Miss Laura's mail. It's been coming for over three years now. Miss Laura was the spinster-lady who lived in my downstairs duplex before me, until the day she passed away. Her spinster-sister lived upstairs, and as near as I can glean from stories the neighbors tell, she died about five years before Miss Laura. (Believe me, I *do* see the irony. My upstairs neighbor is also a single woman—but I'm thinking there *must* be another way out of here.)

Her sister's mail has stopped. But Miss Laura's keeps coming.

There's no family member to forward the mail to, and so I destroy it. But having collected it for quite a while, I've learned things about Miss Laura, even though we never met.

She was a supporter of the Houston Livestock Show and Rodeo and probably a stockholder in two corporations, whose annual reports she still receives. I know which political party she favored—or the one she must have written at least one check to. She still gets two Christmas cards each year, so someone out there is as bad a list-keeper as I am—maybe worse. And she once ordered cosmetics from France that most certainly got lost in transit, since they arrived a good two years after her death.

It's strange to have these odd reminders of Miss Laura arrive on my doorstep. But I don't want them to stop. Since there doesn't seem to be anyone to remember her, I'm glad to do so every now and then.

Someday, someone will get my mail. And if they get it long enough, they'll know things about me too. They'll know what catalogs I favored and which magazines I read.

They'll see who didn't remove me from their Christmas card list, and when my dog was due for shots.

Even if I don't leave a family behind, I hope there'll be more than just my mail to be remembered by.

I hope someone keeps my love of words and takes my books and journals and notebooks out every now and then to peruse their pages. I hope the box of recipes in my kitchen (some of them in my grandmother's handwriting) finds its way into another cook's hands and results in years of lovely smells and nourishing meals. I hope I leave true laughter, and deep insight, and bits and pieces of bright, blazing truth that someone tucks away and saves.

But most of all, I want to leave plenty of Jesus and of his joy. And I want that joy to keep coming, over and over again, just the way it's come to me.

And Jesus said to them, "Therefore every scribe who has become a disciple of the kingdom of heaven is like a head of a household, who brings out of his treasure things new and old."

Matthew 13:52

I want to leave a legacy, don't you? What would you like to be remembered for? What sorts of treasure, new and old, do you hope your memory brings forth when you are gone?

A Midweek Deli Drama

I was having lunch alone in a tiny, neighborhood spot where the tables are so close to one another you can't help but overhear several other conversations. I was quite content with my book and salad and trying to tune everything else out, but less than three feet away an impossible-to-ignore drama was unfolding.

Two women were loudly dissecting the domestic dilemma of the younger of the two. Her teenagers didn't respect "Darrell." (Not the name she used.) The friction was especially bad between him and her son. Hers were good kids, she stated—and she had been a good mother under difficult circumstances. (Ugly divorce implied.)

"It's not my kids," she explained to her lunch partner. "It's him. If my kids weren't good kids my son wouldn't be the captain of his soccer team, and my daughter wouldn't be a cheerleader."

I'm glad I wasn't her lunch partner. I might have needed to interject something here, and she wasn't *nearly* through talking.

She and "Darrell" were in counseling. Her counselor said, "forget him." She wasn't ready for that. He didn't have a job. He wasn't paying any of their bills. Apparently he wasn't her current spouse, either. She didn't like how he had treated her on their recent "family" vacation. And she couldn't understand why her kids didn't respect the relationship. (Another "Duh!" moment that was charitably ignored by her mostly silent companion.)

I tried to focus on my salad and stuffed the urge to stand up, take two steps over to their table, and say, "Oh, sweetie. Let's review here."

I have been (fairly, I fear) accused of having the not-so-spiritual gift of "selective mercy," which is probably worse than having no mercy at all. "Selective mercy" means if I think you are not responsible for your rotten, miserable circumstances I have lots of mercy, but if it seems to me that you're contributing to them, little or none.

I didn't have to hear much more to decide that this woman was throwing a nonstop party at which disaster was the invited guest of honor. I closed my book, placed my napkin on the table, and left. And for the rest of the day (and several days after) I thought about her.

In less than five minutes it was clear to me that her choices were her problem. She was reaping what she had sowed and what she continued to sow. That's how it works.

But here's the hard part: *I do that too.* And at times I can be just as blind to my role in my own discomfort as she was to hers. The only difference is, I have to work harder at it. Because the Spirit of Truth has taken up residence in my heart and is quick to put a finger on my foolish, destructive behavior whenever it occurs.

She didn't know the truth—and so couldn't be expected to follow it. I do. To deliberately disregard it is far more foolish than to stumble around in the darkness. And to fail to share it is utterly and completely unkind.

"Then you will know the truth, and the truth will set you free."

John 8:32 NIV

If you know the truth, you have a responsibility to walk in the truth's light. So do I. To fail to do so is to bargain for no small amount of heartbreak. The truth you and I know is the truth that we obey. And that's the truth that finally sets us free.

Night (and Day)

I saw him sitting on the curb with his skateboard wedged under his knees as I approached the stop sign and almost immediately decided he must be waiting there for a bus. He looked about sixteen . . . brown skin, dreadlockedhair, baggy sweatpants, and a basketball jersey that probably hung below his knees when he stood. He would have looked less out of place in my part of town than he did in the neighborhood I was driving through.

As I slowed to a stop I might have simply stared straight ahead, filing his image away in my mind under "kid alone at dusk, waiting for a bus," except for one thing. He was reading a book. Reading intently, and shaping the words with his lips as though saying them out loud might make them easier to follow. And the book he was reading was a paperback copy of Elie Wiesel's *Night*.

His choice of summer reading surprised me. *Night* is by no means light fare.

> *God made man because He loves stories . . .*
> Elie Wiesel

Except for the book, he would have quickly disappeared from view and from my mind. But what skater-kid with wild hair and time on his hands willingly reads a holocaust memoir/novel—even one told from the perspective of a fifteen-year-old boy? It was the book that kept me thinking of him. It didn't seem to fit the person I'd pegged him to be. Sure, maybe it was on his reading list for junior English at his high school. But it's July, for Pete's sake. Plenty of time for further procrastination. And he wasn't on the first page. He was into it. Way in.

He was reading a story of a young man who experienced incredible suffering in a place so wretched that it convinced him God could not exist. Maybe this skater-kid's circumstances were crushing and bleak too. Maybe he identified with the teenaged protagonist's pain as he witnessed the horror of Auschwitz and wondered each day if death would come for him, as it had come for the rest of his family before his very eyes.

If you're looking for deeper meaning here, I'm not sure there is any. But I'm pretty sure of this: I judge strangers too quickly and on far too little data. I don't know as much as I pretend to. And if I were to look carefully enough, often enough, I might glimpse the doorway into someone's true story and linger long enough to hear the rest of the tale.

I don't want the kid I saw to conclude that God is dead. And I don't want to conclude that it wouldn't matter if he did. Because the difference between looking at something and really seeing is like the difference between night and day.

For God, who said, "Light shall shine out of darkness," is the One who has shone in our hearts to give the Light of the knowledge of the glory of God in the face of Christ.

2 Corinthians 4:6

Whom have you overlooked or ignored simply because you thought at a glance you knew all about them that there was to know? You don't. I don't. There's more to each of us than meets the eye. Take the time to look and listen to the people around you. They're far from ordinary, and each one has a unique story to tell.

Pomp and Circumstance

Every spring, one or two plump, fine-papered commencement invitations come hand-addressed to me, but this year there were none. No high school or college graduates were among my circle of family, friends, and children-of-friends—

so this year I missed hearing "Pomp and Circumstance." But I didn't miss graduation.

At a business contact's invitation—before our scheduled meeting—I slipped into the graduation celebration ("ceremony" falls short of the right word) at a local shelter's transitional living community. There were fewer than one hundred people in the room, but when I arrived, jubilant music was filling it to the brim.

And these graduates weren't the somber, mechanical sort, either. They were robed in unmatched blue and gold and burgundy, and they marched as a group to a stage facing the audience—but that's where their similarity to other graduates I've observed ended.

They weren't eighteen or twenty-two . . . most were older, and looked it. They weren't candidates for degrees in chemistry or physics or English, or even high school diplomas. The courses they had completed had names like ARK Parenting, New Hope Drug Treatment, Building Better Families, and Anger Management. And these thirty-one candidates had something the majority of graduates I see these days mostly seem to lack: the unchecked joy of achievement and a sense that they were on the brink of something big.

Several of them spoke—most nervously—but none of them came close to putting me to sleep. They didn't pepper their words with platitudes or tired clichés, either. One opened her brief address by explaining how she'd come to this place: "My parole officer said it was four years in prison or rehab, and I chose rehab."

Two spoke of their desire to become nurses. One recovering addict wanted to become a chemical dependency counselor. One said she was a great cook and hoped to one day own a B&B that served "the best home-cooked food in town." One wished her mother had lived long enough to see her graduate. One said he planned to be "a rock and roll drummer for Jesus." And why not?

When they struggled with their words or their emotions, their fellow graduates and residents encouraged them. "That's all right," they'd offer. "Take your time. Come on now." I wasn't around to see how this matriculating class began their journey at Star of Hope. But I was privileged to see how they were ending this portion of it. They were being changed from the inside out, and whatever had come before only made this day even sweeter for the ride.

At commencement's end, the traditional "Pomp and Circumstance" was replaced with a rousing rendition of Myrna Summers's "We're Gonna Make It," accompanied with enthusiasm on a slightly-out-of-tune, upright piano: Call *me* a believer.

> "For I know the plans that I have for you," declares the LORD, "plans for welfare and not for calamity to give you a future and a hope."
>
> Jeremiah 29:11

A friend of mine working on his doctoral dissertation mentioned that when he is awarded his degree, he probably won't even attend the ceremony. He doesn't see it as a cause for celebration, as such. But these graduates had achieved (by the world's standards, anyway) far less, and they were thrilled to celebrate and share it. Is there a milestone in your life that you've neglected to celebrate? Why not do it today?

Death Defeated!

The day dawned cold and wet in my town. It's supposed to rain all day. And truthfully, the world (or my tiny corner of it) looks just like it did yesterday morning, and the morning before.

But it's not.

It's not the same at all, because two days ago, my best friend's father died. The weather's the same, but the world is different, because a good man who lived a good life is now living a shiny new version of it somewhere else.

Well-chosen words have already been written and will long be spoken about Bud. They will be true. He was a kind and committed husband for over fifty years. A veteran of World War II. A public servant in our city for decades. He raised two daughters and a son with the beautiful, porcelain-skinned wife of his youth and cared for her faithfully until she passed through the doorway of death without him.

He loved golf and good books and Southern gospel; he knew his neighbors and they knew him. He enjoyed other people's children and Texas Longhorn football—and he ended his days where he wanted most to be: at home, in the tiny frame house he built himself, where all the best stuff that had ever happened to him happened.

I don't know what this morning's headline will be. But I know what it should be. In the tallest type—the size reserved for wars and elections and stunning national disasters, it should read "DEATH DEFEATED!" It will be a travesty if it does not.

And the subhead should read: "Well done, thou good and faithful servant." Because every time a child of his dies, the Son of God's stunning victory is reenacted. Since he himself took the beating and deserted the lonely tomb, death is no longer a dead end for us. Because he goes and prepares us a place, what used to be a prison is a prized destination instead. "DEATH DEFEATED!"

We weep on this side. And it's right that we should. But on the other side, the Savior throws back his beautiful head and laughs the laugh of Lazarus at a harmless foe that has no fangs. And he spreads his arms wide, showing the ancient love marks on his palms, and folds in an eternal embrace each one who belongs to him. Our loss is heaven's gain.

I see the paper on the driveway. And in a moment, I'll retrieve it. When I unfold it, I'm sure I'll see that they've gotten it wrong. That the story to end all stories has been ignored. But only here. Only now. Where time isn't, and where Jesus is enthroned, the news of the day is the same news every day: "DEATH DEFEATED."

Hallelujah and amen.

> My sheep recognize my voice. I know them, and they
> follow me. I give them real and eternal life . . . No one
> can steal them from out of my hand.
>
> John 10:27–29 Message

Every name in today's obituaries is the name of an eternal being. Those who have placed their faith in Jesus will be welcomed into his beautiful presence forever. For the believer, death has already been defeated, and nothing in this world—or the world to come—can make it stick.

God's Work and Good Tables

It's certain that God's work is not shoddily produced. He pronounced *all* that he created good—and it was. Dorothy Sayers once rightly suggested that our own work "must be good work before it can call itself God's work." But good work is often no more than simple work, faithfully and lovingly repeated.

I was reminded of the lasting value of good, simple work not long ago, when a childhood friend of mine died. His name was Bob Keeshan, but I knew him for years as Captain Kangaroo. We met each morning through the magic of television—he in a conductor's coat with deep pockets, a cap set on top of his bowl haircut, and mustachioed face—me in my footie pajamas and bed hair, holding a bowl of Fruit Loops and milk in two hands.

He had friends, and he introduced me to them: Tom Terrific, Mr. Green Jeans, Mr. Moose, and a great, sleeping grandfather clock. I knew him in black and white, but his simple work colored my world. I came to love animals, and rhymes, and even getting up early (still a habit today) through my good friend the Captain.

He didn't wow me with special effects (there weren't any in his repertoire). He didn't even teach in the clever way that *Sesame Street* would inform the generation after mine. He just showed up, morning after morning, day after day, for over thirty years, doing the kind of good work that he enjoyed. And I wasn't the only child who loved him for it.

Captain Kangaroo's career (and a recent, welcome change in my own working life) has made me think again about my responsibility as a believer to do good work. It was also Dorothy Sayers who said, "The very first demand that his religion should make upon a carpenter is that he should make good tables. No crooked table legs or ill-fitting drawers ever, I dare say, came out of the carpenter's shop at Nazareth."[2]

When I remarked to my sister that for the first time in twenty-three years I was not reporting to someone, she stunned me with this: "Leigh, you're working for the same One you've always worked for. Nothing's changed." She was right. I have the same boss and the same charge as ever: to faithfully, lovingly do good work. To make good tables, to the glory of the One who made me.

Thanks, Lynn. Thanks, Captain. I'm off to the shop for another honest day's work.

Do your best. Work from the heart for your real Master, for God, confident that you'll get paid in full when you come into your inheritance. Keep in mind always that the ultimate Master you're serving is Christ. The sullen servant who does shoddy work will be held responsible. Being a follower of Jesus doesn't cover up bad work.

Colossians 3:23–25 Message

Could anyone tell from the quality of your work that you labor from the heart for your real Master? How different would your efforts look if you embraced that truth? How faithful would you be to your calling if the Son of God signed your paycheck?

"Daddy's Got You!"

As kids go, I was only an average risk taker. I didn't leap off the roof of the house, or race through busy intersections on my bike, or swallow giant jawbreakers whole. But I was ready for almost any challenge that was preceded by these three words: "Daddy's got you."

I heard them as I rode my training-wheel-less bike down the driveway for the first time, and leaped—eyes and nose squeezed shut—into the deep end of the Quintana Oil Company swimming pool in Refugio, Texas. The words weren't audible at other fear-filled events, but I was still certain of them when I stood at the free throw line in my first junior high basketball game, bawled my way through a newly broken heart at sixteen, and watched my parents drive away from my college dorm the fall of my freshman year.

Knowing that someone who loves you "has your back" can go a long way to making you brave. It did me.

I wonder how many things I would never have tried without my dad's constant, encouraging presence. I wonder how often I would have waited in the shadows and hoped for someone else to lead if he hadn't told me I could. My dad who made me brave did the bravest thing for me when I turned thirteen. He wrote me a letter (delivered with a long-stemmed red rose) that celebrated my short life with typical parental enthusiasm, and ended it with words something like this: "Your mother and I will always be proud of you, but it is your Maker you must answer to, and yourself you will see in the mirror each day. Many things may change, but one will remain constant: your Dad's love for his daughter."

Early on, my dad set me free from pleasing him so that I might fully follow Jesus—and the dreams *he* had placed in my very young heart. That is why it has been no great leap of faith for me, in the days since, to believe without undue questioning the bold promises and commands from my heavenly Father's book. He says he will never forsake me. I count on that. He says I am justified and have peace with him. I rest in that peace. He says I can do all things through Christ who strengthens me, so I am confident that it is so. He says he is with me always. And most days, his promises make me better, and braver, than I am.

Put me like a seal over your heart, like a seal on your arm. For love is as strong as death, jealousy is as severe as Sheol; its flashes are flashes of fire, the very flame of the LORD. Many waters cannot quench love, nor will rivers overflow it.

Song of Solomon 8:6–7

What would you attempt today if you were certain that your loving Abba Father had your back? Then believe it. Daddy's got you!

Of Spiderman and Kings

Peter Parker didn't *ask* to be Spiderman. He was a slightly geeky teenager who received a spider bite and discovered he had "gifts" that other high school sophomores didn't. He could spin webs from his fingertips. And defy gravity. All good stuff when your previous strong suit was chemistry, and you never got the girl. But Peter didn't immediately become a superhero. That took time . . . and tragedy.

His beloved uncle was killed in a street crime that Peter might have prevented. As a result of this heartbreaking loss, he began to use his unplanned powers fighting evil for the good of mankind.

Peter Parker didn't ask to be Spiderman, and shepherd-boy David never asked to be a king. He was selected from a lineup of likelier siblings by the prophet Samuel when he was just a teenager. Then he spent years in an odd training program: running for his life from the misguided man he was destined to replace.

But when word came that King Saul had died, the young man-who-would-be-king did not celebrate. He grieved: "Then David took hold of his clothes and tore them, and so also did all the men who were with him. They mourned and wept and fasted until evening for Saul and his son Jonathan and for the people of the LORD and the house of Israel, because they had fallen by the sword" (2 Sam. 1:11–12).

Peter and David both learned the hard way that with power and chosen-ness come responsibility . . . and that there's more to a leader than his public performance. Leaders are made in private—and just putting on the crown doesn't make a man a king any more than putting on the blue and red leotard made a nerdy schoolboy a superhero.

Peter was a hero because of his heart. And David was a great king because of his heart for God. He so identified with God and his interests that he didn't even view Saul's death as gain—he saw it as a tragic end to the flawed man that God had placed in power over David and all of Israel.

Perhaps you're thinking that you're more Peter Parker than Spiderman. More shepherd boy than king. That you're rather ordinary at best and certainly not marked for greatness. Oh—but you are wrong! You and I are *more* than superheroes or kings! We are sons and daughters—joint heirs with Christ and image bearers of the King of Kings.

It is not enough for us to "put on the uniform" and go through the prescribed motions of worship, devotion, service, and prayer—or to simply live a "cleaner" life than the man or woman next door. We must be changed . . . in private and from the inside out. Because power doesn't make a man. Power *reveals* a man.

For you are all sons of God through faith in Christ Jesus.

Galatians 3:26

There's a lot of Peter Parker in me. I'm not a likely hero or an eager one. But God is in the process of transforming me through the power of his Spirit so that I might live beyond the ordinary for his glory. (Just don't ask to see me fly.)

The Things That Julia Moves

I'm a late adapter. I don't typically jump on the bandwagon first and set the trend. I finally got a microwave in 2001 . . . grudgingly. I watched my black-and-white TV until it was mostly white, then it really *did* "fade to black." Until very recently I didn't own a DVD or anything to play one on. And I was the last of my friends to get a maid.

A few months ago, while I was deep into a major project at the office and working on a book manuscript at night—I realized my cleaning was leaving something to be desired. When my upstairs neighbor mentioned that her maid, Julia, was looking for another client, I took that as a "sign." Julia took on the downstairs half of the 1938 duplex where I live, coming every third week to do the basics. (Not the laundry or the dishes, Mom—I still do those myself. Often.)

When I walked through the front door the first Thursday that Julia cleaned, I breathed in the smell of pine and admired the fresh sheen on the wooden floors, the scrubbed spotless tub, and plumped sofa pillows. It was all good. Very good.

Then I noticed that some things had moved. The rugs were straight, but definitely off their previous mark. The paper-towel holder had migrated several inches from its regular spot on the kitchen counter. The ottoman in the living room was sitting at a jaunty new angle. As lovely as it was to walk into a freshly cleaned house—it was a little disconcerting to see my things in a place *I* hadn't put them.

At first.

But then I realized that I *liked* the ottoman facing southeast instead of southwest. And that the kitchen rugs worked just as well horizontally as they had vertically. Now I look forward to every third Thursday not just because I know the house will be spotless, but because I'll have the pleasure of looking for the things that Julia moves and seeing if I like them better that way.

Do you ever feel that when you get your life arranged well, God moves something? That's the thing about him. He takes liberties. Maybe a favorite "piece" will turn up missing and then reappear in another, better location. Or a familiar pattern will be disrupted but ultimately improved. It's hard to keep everything in the place you first put it when the Creator of the universe decides to come in and make himself at home—but that is good. *Very* good. Because becoming settled in our own security is never better than being surprised by Almighty God.

And at least once a month now, I have Julia—and the things she moves—to remind me.

> "Do not call to mind the former things, or ponder things of the past. Behold, I will do something new, now it will spring forth; will you not be aware of it? I will even make a roadway in the wilderness, rivers in the desert."
>
> Isaiah 43:18–19

Has God moved something that you've become accustomed to seeing in a certain way? Are you irritated by that? Disoriented? And is your aversion to change (or your need for control) interfering with your ability to see what new thing he might be doing—and how it might be better than before?

Horse Holders, Handlers, and Other Hangers-on

A fellow I once worked with later became the press secretary for a very powerful political figure—someone you'd know if I "dropped" the name. (I won't.) He and I were hired on the same day to do similar jobs at a large law firm. He went on, apparently to greater things. (I just went on.)

My former co-worker handled the affairs of people with influence—and that made him a person of some influence as well. Because when powerful people limit those who have direct access to them, the ones who do are somehow elevated to a special status of their own.

It's odd, isn't it, that one of the hallmarks of power is distance? Few people who have achieved notoriety or power are without "horse-holders," handlers, and other hangers-on. They seem to come with the territory. The powerful don't fly coach. They have limos. Drivers. Schedulers. Personal assistants. They occupy corner offices and frequent executive washrooms. They don't answer their own phones. Ever. Many rarely place their own outgoing calls.

So, how did the busiest, most in-demand, most powerful person who ever lived deal with the pressures and pulls of notoriety? He got twelve men to travel with him. But they weren't bodyguards or handlers. He called them friends. Sometimes they got confused about their role and tried to "screen" out the nobodies who hungered for their boss's eye—but he seldom stood for it. He welcomed children. He spoke to "questionable" women in public. He ate with tax collectors and sinners. He let sick men and women reach out and touch him without worrying about infection (or lawsuits). And when they tried to protect him from the soldiers who finally came to arrest him, he presented himself openly. He didn't hide behind anyone—not even those who would have gladly "covered" for him.

I'm not a powerful person. I probably shouldn't be. I think coach is a tad confining, and I could quickly adapt to first class. I don't have a secretary, but I sometimes employ caller ID in a defensive mode. And the idea of my own ladies' room doesn't sound too bad.

But if I ever *did* become a person of influence, I pray I'd remember this: the One who should have denied me access gave it. The One who could have refused my call took it. The One who by all rights could have demanded my death gave me life. And today—right now—he'll hear my request without a handler standing between us.

Now isn't that something?

> Think of yourselves the way Christ Jesus thought of himself. He had equal status with God but didn't think so much of himself that he had to cling to the advantages of that status no matter what. Not at all. When the time came, he set aside the privileges of deity and took on the status of a slave, became *human*! Having become human, he stayed human. It was an incredibly humbling process. He didn't claim special privileges.
>
> Philippians 2:5–7 Message

Insulation is tempting, isn't it? There's something comforting in knowing you have a buffer to employ when the world draws too near and demands too much. Jesus traveled with an entourage, yes. But he was far, far more attuned to their needs than they were to his.

Written on Her Forehead

*H*er name was Grace. (It really was.) I met her in a church reception hall amidst the sounds of laughter and happy conversation, and she was lovely. Her husband introduced himself first and then stepped aside slightly for her to do the same. She angled her petite body in front of his, looked into my face, with one hand clasped mine, and with the other drew an invisible line across her forehead, as if she was pointing to a single word on a tablet.

"Stroke," she said to me carefully and slowly.

We were a pair, Grace and me. She couldn't speak, and I didn't know what to say. She wanted to greet me—and I wanted to know her. At least as much of her as the next few moments could afford. But first she had to tell me that she wouldn't be carrying her end of the conversation, at least not in the usual way. So Grace held my hand and smiled up into my face with eyes that said, "I have a million stories, and I can't tell a single of them anymore. But I'm glad you're here, and I love you."

I heard her clearly. I swear I did.

She glowed with love and grace and beauty . . . and she reached out to me, even though it was awkward for her to do so. She told her own story, written on her forehead. She didn't ask anyone else to tell it for her. She didn't pretend it was any different than it was.

Maybe because Grace couldn't talk, I felt a need to economize with words too. I think I only said a couple myself, then I hugged her and kissed the pretty gray curls that framed her face. We had a conversation. You just couldn't hear it.

I've thought about that meeting for a long while. Wouldn't it be easier, in a way, if we all had our stories written on our foreheads? Then our conversations could be placed in context, and the chances for misunderstanding one another would be reduced. The problem is, some of us would have stories far less lovely than Grace's written there. On any given day, my story might read "self-centered," or "too-busy-to-be-bothered," or "nursing a grudge." Or "grieving," or "frightened," or "lonely."

What about yours?

When Moses instructed the sons of Israel as the Lord commanded him, he even suggested something similar. "These commandments that I give you today are to be upon your hearts. . . . Tie them as symbols on your hands and bind them on your foreheads" (Deut. 6:6, 8 NIV). In other words, what God has done inside should be as visible (to us and to others) as a sign on our forehead. God had done great things for his children. He wanted them to remember those things, and remember him. Then when others saw his people coming, he wanted them to know their story . . . as easily as if it were written on their foreheads.

> You shall fear the LORD your God; you shall serve Him and cling to Him, and you shall swear by His name. He is your praise and He is your God, who has done these great and awesome things for you which your eyes have seen."
>
> Deuteronomy 10:20–21

So what's your sign say? Beloved? Remembered? Healed? Blessed? Forgiven? There's a truer story than you know that is written on your forehead . . . and on mine.

"My Name Is Dulcinea"

I don't know if seeing *Man of La Mancha* on Broadway is akin to a religious experience for most people, but it was for me. From the first notes of flamenco music on a single guitar—I breathed deep and prepared myself for enchantment . . . and I was not disappointed.

The stage revival of Cervantes' story of knight errant Don Quixote is full of idealism and energy—but at its heart, it's a story of redemption. The knight changes everyone he meets for the better, and he changes no one more completely than the woman he adoringly calls Dulcinea.

She is Aldonza to the rest of the world, weary and heart-hardened, with no illusions about her condition: "I was spawned in a ditch by a mother who left me there, naked and cold and too hungry to cry; I never blamed her. I'm sure she left hoping that I'd have the good sense to die!"

But Don Quixote, from the moment he sees her, calls Aldonza "my lady," and looks at her through the redeeming eyes of love: "I have dreamed thee too long, never seen thee or touched thee. But known thee with all of my heart. Half a prayer, half a song, thou hast always been with me, though we have been always apart."

Then, in a voice full of the reverence she is sure she does not deserve, he tells her who she really is: "Dulcinea . . . Dulcinea . . . I see heaven when I see thee, Dulcinea. And thy name is like a prayer an angel whispers . . . Dulcinea . . . Dulcinea!"

She tries to correct him. She insists she's not Dulcinea but Aldonza. She is coarse. He is tender. She swears and spits and mocks his vision of a purity she never knew. "Take the clouds from your eyes," she tells him, "and see me as I really am! I am no one! I am nothing! I'm only Aldonza the whore!" But even as she protests, she can't put out of her mind the thought that someone—even a half-crazy knight—sees the woman she *could* be . . . the woman she's too afraid to hope to be. And God help her, the woman she still longs to be.

When Don Quixote lies on his deathbed, Aldonza comes to him. She begs him to remember her, to call her by her other name. But he dies, and in his death, something inside her changes forever. Another mourner at the knight's bedside moves to comfort her, calling her "Aldonza." She straightens herself and says to him with firm conviction: "My name . . . is Dulcinea." Don Quixote's love had made her the woman she was always meant to be.

> But you are the ones chosen by God, chosen for the high calling of priestly work, chosen to be a holy people, God's instruments to do his work and speak out for him, to tell others of the night-and-day difference he made for you—from nothing to something, from rejected to accepted.
>
> 1 Peter 2:9–10 Message

How tender of God to call us by a lovelier name than our own, until by faith we can assume our true identity! Have you heard him whisper another, more beautiful name to you?

No-Matter-What Love

*D*ana Reeve had cancer and she died. She was forty-four and beautiful, a widow who'd lost a huge part of her famous husband more than a decade earlier, and the precious sum of him not many months before her own diagnosis. Hers was the glowing face pressed next to his in photographs; she was the brave foot soldier in his public, determined fight to forge on against staggering disability. They were a storybook team, and the world applauded their beauty and resolve. She lost her husband and then she was lost. They left behind a teenaged son.

Dana's death made national headlines. Quickly assembled video montages chronicled the public parts of her lovely too-short life. Celebrities from New York to Hollywood to Capitol Hill mourned her passing, and talking-head physicians took occasion to instruct on her cancer and his spinal cord injuries.

The world took note as if to say, "She counted."

Less than forty-eight hours before Dana's death, cancer claimed another woman. Her name was Cass. She wasn't young or beautiful or selfless or famous. She wasn't even particularly winsome or her ways inviting. She didn't have the world pulling for her or the financial resources to command the best care for her disease. No one who learned of her diagnosis said, "It just isn't fair," or asked, "How could God let that happen?" She had no family nearby and no lifelong friends to love her through her passing.

But she was by no means alone.

In her small church of a few hundred souls, Cass counted. Everyone knew her, and probably one in ten had participated in some tangible way in her care. She was prayed over, encouraged, driven to appointments and moved countless times. She had advocates and caregivers, helpers and sitters. She received what she needed, whether it was a meal or a pair of eyeglasses, a place for her possessions or a place to die.

As a community, we celebrated her home-going. And no one who celebrated denied her tendency to be demanding or cranky, or tried to pretend that she was easy to love. She wasn't. But she was loved with no-matter-what love. God loved her well, and so his people simply followed his example. Because those who are God's are called to care for the least, the last, and the lost, just as much as for the beautiful and the blessed.

The papers didn't say who was with Dana Reeve as she died, but I know who guided Cass through those last steps to her truest home. She had a beautiful Bridegroom who loved her, no matter what—and today he is loving her still.

> For while we were still helpless, at the right time Christ died for the ungodly. For one will hardly die for a righteous man; though perhaps for the good man someone would dare even to die. But God demonstrates His own love toward us, in that while we were yet sinners, Christ died for us.
>
> Romans 5:6–8

Is there someone in your life who isn't easy to love? That's all right. Neither were you and I, and God loved us anyway. His Word says, "We love, because He first loved us" (1 John 4:19). He asks us to imitate him and to do as he has done.

Part 3

Ordinary Things

Awaiting New Wine

*I*t's time for a new Bible. Not because at least a dozen new versions of the world's oldest bestseller are introduced each year and begging to be tried but because mine is falling apart. I don't *want* a new Bible. The one I've used for a decade now is comfortable, well-marked, and familiar. I am in no way eager to break in a spotless, creaseless, pristine cousin of my beloved, beat-up companion . . . but I'm going to have to, soon.

The cover has detached itself from the spine, and pages are coming unhinged great sections at a time. The concordance has several folded pages stashed in the back, the way my grandmother used to keep folded tissues in her purse. If I don't turn its pages gently and coddle it carefully in my lap, it might not last another week.

But I don't want to let it go.

I don't want to let it go because a new Bible always feels like starting over, and one glance at this one reminds me I've come a very long way. I know the tear-stained pages where my heart has been broken, and the pages that have felt like sweet balm to the wounds this world can't help but make. I know where to turn, within a page or two, to the verses that have shaped my life the way a blacksmith shapes steel—and even though I know them by heart, I love seeing them in print and reading them again and again. I know where the promises lie that feed my soul . . . and I need them no less now than I did when this Bible was my "new" one.

I'm reluctant to retire it because it's not just any book, or even any Bible. It's my history with Jesus for the last ten years, and it's unspeakably sweet to me. The thought of fresh pages and temporary fumbling isn't compelling—so I've put off the inevitable for another day.

My reluctance to replace my old Bible is in some ways like my reluctance to leave whatever comfort God has given me and venture into the newness of the unknown. But he didn't call me to a faith that stalls out in the first place it finds that feels like home. He called—and calls—me on.

There is infinitely more ahead with him than there ever was behind. The past, as sweet and hard fought and precious as it was, is not where I am meant to live. Every day with him is a clean, white page waiting for old words to be applied in new ways. He will do a thing . . . bring new wine . . . teach new lessons . . . if I will let go of the old.

So when no one's looking, one day soon, I'll kiss the cover of this dear old friend and put it away. And I'll crack the spine and breathe in the smell of fresh new pages . . . and wait again for brand-new wine.

"No one puts new wine into old wineskins; otherwise the wine will burst the skins, and the wine is lost, and the skins as well; but one puts new wine into fresh wineskins."

Mark 2:22

I like change, but I can still be found clinging to familiar comforts. Keeping an old Bible past its prime is one thing, but refusing to go on with God because I've become lazy, complacent, or satisfied is another. He means to stretch my comfortable boundaries in every way they can be stretched—and I mean to let him. Do you?

"Six-Foot Frosty Seeks Same . . ."

*O*utdoor holiday decorations have become huge. Literally. Already reindeer are grazing in half the yards on my block, and oversized Peanuts characters are assembled and caroling two houses down. My next-door neighbor's lighted lawn figures move their heads from side to side; they nearly frightened me to death the first time I saw them stir.

But the character most frequently spotted this season is an enormous, inflatable snowman that looks like a cross between the Michelin tire guy and a giant marshmallow. He must be at least six feet tall, with his arms stretched out wide as if offering a hug. I counted half a dozen of these "Frosties" within a few blocks of each other, all reaching out to empty air with more of their kind very near but not connecting. Not touching.

Sometimes that's what Christmas feels like.

We're smiling. Our arms are open wide. But it's mostly exterior decoration. Outdoor stuff. We pass within feet or yards of each other, but we don't quite meet—at least in ways that are real and warm. I imagine somehow introducing all the "Frosties" in my neighborhood one night, so they could at least congregate in the wee hours while we sleep. "Six-foot Frosty seeks same," their snowman personal ads might say. "No baggage. Loves cold starlit nights." Call me silly. I'd like to connect them for the holidays.

At my house, the decorations are on the inside . . . and they're not huge. Yesterday I set my tiny nativity set on my desk between the computer screen and keyboard, because that's where I'll see it most often. It's less than eight inches square, and all of its characters are glued in. The baby Jesus's manger is no bigger than a walnut, but as I put it out this year, I noticed something I hadn't seen before: his infant arms are spread open wide, just like Frosty's. All eyes are on him. Mary, Joseph, the three wise men, and the donkey are all looking his way, and his arms are stretched out to them just the same way they would be thirty-three years after his birth.

When I look at it, I can't help but reach out too and place my fingertip between his arms where it fits perfectly. *This is my Father's world*, I think—the true, tiny, tender one. And touching this small baby reminds me to connect with him. To run to the place where I belong. Between his arms is the one place I am sure to be at home.

> Then a shoot will spring from the stem of Jesse, and a branch from his roots will bear fruit. The Spirit of the LORD will rest on Him, the spirit of wisdom and understanding, the spirit of counsel and strength, the spirit of the knowledge and the fear of the LORD.
>
> Isaiah 11:1–2

God didn't come in the flesh to wow us. He didn't need to. He came to win us—and in the most unlikely of ways. The God of the universe "downsized" for you and me, so that we could connect—now and forever—with him. Aren't you glad that he did?

Sanctification and Bathroom Rugs

I've learned a little something about what it means to be sanctified from the three rugs in my bathroom. Two are small and square, and one is long and narrow. (It's a long and narrow bathroom.) I bought the rugs because they felt good on my feet. They're thick and tan, with loopy pile that looked perfect in the store. They looked perfect in my bathroom too, for about a day and a half. They would have had that store-aisle perfect look for much longer, had I not walked on them.

But a long, narrow bathroom gets long, narrow traffic and—like everybody else—I step from the shower with wet feet. One rug was meant to absorb that water, and it does. But *as* it does, its thick pile gets damp . . . and flat. And as the days go by, the rugs look less and less inviting although they still do their job quite well.

While I wish the rugs could look pristine all the time, it is, after all, a bathroom . . . and the only one in the house. So when it's just me at home, I don't bother too much with their flatness. But when I'm expecting company I alter my routine.

When guests are coming over, I take the rugs to the clothes dryer, toss in a couple of softener sheets for good measure, and fluff them for half an hour or more. They come out looking brand new. Then I carry them to the bathroom and arrange them in their regular pattern on the floor. And (this is the funny part) I try to avoid stepping on them at all until my guests arrive.

Like a kid playing sidewalk hopscotch I maneuver myself in and out of the bathroom, never touching the rugs. I don't want to flatten them or leave footprints. I step instead on the cold tiles the rugs were made to buffer me from. I shift my focus from utility to appearance for the benefit (or so I tell myself) of others, on the offhand chance they might be offended by flat rugs. The last time I did this I realized the sheer ridiculousness of not using something that was meant to be used for fear it would look . . . used.

Do you ever try, as you follow Christ, to make it look effortless? Do you seek to serve him with every hair artfully in place? Do you hope to be greatly used by God but never worn thin in the process? I am sanctified—set apart for use—by a good and great King who did not come to

be kept spotless and unsullied in front of "the company."
He wasn't just used. He was utterly used up to his final,
dying breath. And nothing could have pleased him—or
his Father—more.

> Now may the God of peace Himself sanctify you
> entirely; and may your spirit and soul and body be
> preserved complete, without blame at the coming of
> our Lord Jesus Christ. Faithful is He who calls you,
> and He also will bring it to pass.

1 Thessalonians 5:23–24

*If it pleases God to use me for my good and his glory, how
can I protest the sometimes less-than-artful results? May I
be flattened into fruitfulness often . . . no matter who's on
hand to see it.*

The Problem with Paper Gowns

*Y*ou'd think with all the advances in modern health care
and medical technology, they'd have done something by
now about the gowns—besides make them flimsier.

Now, instead of a fabric garment with mysterious openings and oddly placed ties, a patient about to be examined,
x-rayed, or otherwise peered at or prodded receives a folded
paper sack the size of a tall kitchen garbage bag to drape
with, minus the twist tie. Anyone with an ounce of modesty
is out of luck. Anyone who believes they have something
to hide (and isn't that everyone, really?) is sunk.

The problem with paper gowns is that they leave too
little to the imagination. They're revealing, unflattering,
and alarmingly fragile. I was reminded of that on my last

doctor's visit—and reminded too, of how committed I am to cover—and not just in the doctor's office. There's much about my redeemed, renewed, but still-being-refurbished heart I'd like to drape until it's "done." But that might take a while. There are flaws I'd like to layer lots of clothing over and not-quite-healed scars I'd like to camouflage.

It's hard—really hard—to stand still under the bright light of day and be seen the way you are, not the way you wish you were. Adam and Eve discovered that quickly "post-apple," when they realized just how exposed they truly were. Their eyes were opened, we're told, and they knew they were naked. So they sewed themselves coverings of fig leaves to cover up. Before there were paper gowns, there were fig leaves . . . and they didn't seem to do the job much better. Dressed in their make-do foliage, the first flawed man and the first flawed woman weren't so very keen on exposure, either.

Maybe the fact that we're still hiding after all this time is a decent argument against the theory of evolution. And the fact that God is still in the clothing business is an equally compelling argument for mercy and grace. In him we are covered. No—we're better than just "covered." We are richly attired men and women whose great and good God has seen our shame and dressed us . . . perfectly.

> The Lord God made garments of skin for Adam and his wife, and clothed them.
>
> Genesis 3:21

> I will rejoice greatly in the Lord, my soul will exult in my God; for He has clothed me with garments of salvation, He has wrapped me with robes of righteousness.
>
> Isaiah 61:10

It's sobering to realize that God has seen us naked. Sin and shame have stripped us bare, yet in his tenderness, he covers us. He provided animal skins for Adam and Eve—but for us, much more: we enter his presence cleansed and unashamed by a new and living way, the blood of his Son, Jesus. In his eyes, we are never shabbily clothed.

My Window Malfunction

I'd mostly taken for granted the small button on the driver's side armrest of my car—and I realized how much only when it stopped working. This particular button raises and lowers the window electronically, and of course, ceased to work when it was no longer under warranty.

My window malfunction was terribly inconvenient. Communicating with the teller at the bank drive-thru proved an acrobatic near-impossibility. Ordering a soft drink at a fast-food place, ditto. And if I thought I could easily speak to the neighbor who flagged me down as I backed out of my driveway, I had, as my granddad used to say "another think coming." When you can't use the window on the driver's side, you quickly learn to accommodate your handicap.

You stop using the bank drive-thru and opt for the lobby instead. You carry bottled water with you in the car and forgo the soft drink stop when it's 98° in the shade. You use idiotic sign language to tell the woman in the lane next to you who wants directions that you won't be able to help her. And you keep doing these things because (1) you're used to them now; and (2) you know it's going to cost you to fix the real problem.

You see where I'm going with this, don't you?

Sometimes my own sin causes things in my life to stop working. The problem becomes crystal clear, but so does the cost required to remedy it. So I choose to accommodate an annoying or even painful malfunction rather than correct it, because I don't want to expend the energy or resources required to move toward wholeness.

To be even more excruciatingly precise, I don't want to *do* things any differently . . . I just want a different outcome.

I know this is not the way it works. (I actually understand the workings of sin better than electric car windows.) I know the solution to my problem is repentance, and that through repentance I have access to the forgiveness—and power—that make real change possible. I know I have a Savior who has paid for my sin and, if you'll forgive the easy metaphor, that my "warranty" has not expired.

In this case, however, knowing does nothing. Something more than knowing is required of me. How foolish I must look when I go through the physical, mental, and spiritual gymnastics required to accommodate my sin, while the One who would heal me stands by. But I don't think he laughs at my malfunctions. Not even a little. I think they break his heart.

> You are dead to sin and alive to God. That's what Jesus did. That means you must not give sin a vote in the way you conduct your lives. Don't give it the time of day. Don't even run little errands that are connected with that old way of life. . . . Sin can't tell you how to live. After all, you're not living under that old tyranny any longer. You're living in the freedom of God.
>
> Romans 6:11–12, 14 Message

Is there an area of your life that's not working because of sin—and that you've been satisfied to accommodate, or work around? Haven't you tired yet of "running errands" for Satan and of giving sin the deciding vote?

Not a Sparrow Falls

My dog Chester pulled hard on the leash in the direction of a gray lump on the sidewalk. We were on our 5:30 a.m. walk—and at 5:30, sleepy, and without my contacts, I couldn't easily make out what he'd found. As I reined in my curious dog and stumbled forward, I saw that the object of his interest was a bird. And although not a feather looked out of place, the odd angle at which it lay (and its unnatural stillness) confirmed that it was dead.

My heart sank. First at the sight of such a pitiful little thing. Then at the thought that, unless I moved it, it wasn't going anywhere. And because it had fallen in the middle of the sidewalk in front of my house, it would be easily visible from my office window all day long, once my vision improved.

Chester soon lost interest (not much of a hunter, my boy), but I couldn't get the fallen bird out of my mind. It made me sad to know that it was lying there, broken and still. Birds aren't meant to stay on the ground. They're made to fly.

All day long my thoughts strayed to the bird, even though it was not a particularly exceptional specimen. It was common. Dull gray. One just like hundreds of other sparrows that I see every day. But it had landed in my sight line. And because it had, I couldn't forget about it even though I wanted to. I saw the shell of something that was once animated, but the life had gone out of it.

Now here's the odd thing. I couldn't shake the thought of one small, dead bird. And yet, day in and day out, I encounter dead people. Oh, they're all breathing—don't misunderstand. But the vibrant, Spirit-infused life of the living God is missing in them. They're empty shells, divorced from the purpose and passion for which they were made. And I notice them less than I do a lifeless bird on the sidewalk.

Not so my Master. He sees them. Really sees each one. And the pang I felt for the fallen sparrow is multiplied an infinite number of times over in his Father's heart when he does. He's made them—carefully crafted each one—and he means for them to have life with a capital "L." Each one matters to him as if he or she were the *only* one. He can't get their lifelessness out of his mind. So why should it go missing from mine?

> "Are not two sparrows sold for a cent? And yet not one of them will fall to the ground apart from your Father. But the very hairs of your head are all numbered. So do not fear; you are more valuable than many sparrows. Therefore everyone who confesses Me before men, I will also confess him before My Father who is in heaven."
>
> Matthew 10:29–32

I remember the first time I understood as a child that Jesus knew and loved me. I could hardly get over it. But an equally powerful revelation is the truth that he knows you just as well and loves you just as much. Multiply that love by each man and woman on the face of the earth, and you've got something big to ponder. "There are," C. S. Lewis once said, "no ordinary people." Every life is sacred. Every person you and I meet today matters deeply to God. Shouldn't that knowledge change us, somehow?

The Stereographic View

A few years ago while I was in New York City on business, I happened into an antiquarian book show at the 7th Regiment Armory on Park Avenue and 67th. It was a rainy spring afternoon, and with time to spare before an appointment I'd taken a long stroll down Park, looking for nothing in particular. What I found was a little bit of heaven in an unexpected place.

Books for me are something of a vice—and a great hall full of them was sensory overload. I bought an early (but not first) edition of C. S. Lewis's *The Four Loves* and lingered over outrageously priced, mint condition copies of the *Dick and Jane* books I learned to read in kindergarten.

In one of the last vendor's stalls before the exit, a fat brown spine with gold engraving caught my eye. It read *The Travel Lessons on the Life of Jesus*. As I pulled it from the shelf I saw that it wasn't a book at all but a case about five inches deep, filled with an odd collection of thirty-five sepia-colored cards depicting places like the Valley of the Kidron, and Cana in Galilee.

Each card had what looked like two identical images on it, placed side by side. On the back was a description of the scene printed in six different languages. It was like an antique travelogue through the Holy Land, and I instantly adored it. The shop-minder explained that these sets were popular in the late 1800s and early 1900s, and he may have even told me what they were called, but I don't remember that. I just remember being giddy over my quirky find and paying a slightly ridiculous price for the privilege of taking it home.

I didn't get the "full picture" of my purchase until some time later, when, at an antique barn in central Texas, I found an odd little item called a "stereoscope." It looked like an eye mask with a Pinocchio-like wooden extension, and the seller said it was used to view "stereographs"—double photograph-like prints mounted on cardboard in such a way that they produced a three-dimensional image when placed in the extension of the scope.

Oprah would have called it an "aha" moment.

The stereographic view of my old cards was something entirely beyond what I'd previously known. And the odd stereograph and my "Jesus" travel cards were made for each other, even though I'd discovered them thousands of miles and nearly three years apart. They both made much more sense together than they had alone.

Does God ever allow you to connect the dots between two seemingly unrelated things, finally understanding them both as if for the first time? Isn't that kind of stereographic view of life just the absolute *best*?

> I pray that the eyes of your heart may be enlightened, so that you will know what is the hope of His calling, what are the riches of the glory of His inheritance in the saints, and what is the surpassing greatness of His power toward us who believe.
>
> Ephesians 1:18–19

I'm so grateful that God's perspective differs vastly from mine. How good is it to know that he sees what we cannot, where we cannot, and in ways we cannot? If there is something in your life today that doesn't make sense, perhaps the story is not yet finished. Wait expectantly for your heavenly Father to bring the pieces together. You'll be very glad that you did.

Sixty-four-Crayon Life!

The box was goldenrod yellow and bright, bold green: a neat, stiff container with a hinged, flip-open lid. The word "CRAYOLA" was blazoned across the front of it, and inside were sixty-four sharpened, paper-wrapped crayons for coloring. There was even a built-in sharpener, for when the crayons' points began to wear down with steady use.

For a long time, crayons came in rather ordinary packs of eight, but sometime during my elementary school years, a marketing genius decided that if eight was good—eight *times* eight was even better. And my schoolmates and I began to long for the sixty-four-crayon box that went *way* past primary colors with choices like periwinkle and olive and silver and bronze. Once we saw the sixty-four possibilities, being restricted to only eight was agony!

I loved the sixty-four-crayon box. I loved the pretty crayon points perfectly aligned in their neat sections and their spotless paper wraps, not yet torn down for shading purposes. I even loved the smell of wax that wafted up to my nose when the box top was opened: strong and solid and familiar.

But truthfully, there were colors I never used in the sixty-four-crayon box. Although the crayon makers had not limited me, my own choices did. I was never a raw sienna kind of girl, for example, and I didn't care much for silver. These stayed sharp. Others did too. I had my favorites, and I gravitated to them again and again. I never fully explored or exhausted the range of possibilities in my sixty-four-crayon box, and it's possible that, even though I've mostly outgrown coloring, I haven't outgrown my tendency to move my fences in.

Jesus made it clear that he came to give me unlimited, many-hued life: *"I came so they can have real and eternal life,"* he said, *"more and better life than they ever dreamed of"* (John 10:10 Message). But sometimes I don't quite know what to do with that freeing promise. When life rushes at me with all its clamor and noise, sometimes I run for cover and the comfort of my "favorite eight."

I'm not sure what to do with the passion of hot magenta, the stress of chartreuse, or the insistent joy of ultra pink, and so I remove them from my box. Indian red makes me jumpy and lavender moody, so I throw them away too. Navy blue is too stiff and mulberry too sweet, so out they go. And before you know it, my box becomes leaner. My palate is diminished. My colors no longer contrast or complement each other. I go monochrome on my own—but my life-giving Savior/Creator/Artist/Friend would never have it so. He wants to fill the box that I'm so busy emptying. He wants to give me sixty-four-crayon life and to have me wear down every last one before I'm done.

> A slave is a transient, who can't come and go at will. The Son, though, has an established position, the run of the house. So if the Son sets you free, you are free through and through.
>
> John 8:35–36 Message

Have you thinned out the coloring box of your life so much that you're living in safe, somber shades of gray? God never meant for it to be so. What would it take for you to embrace the life he came to give you? How soon could you start?

The Catalog Life

The price of postage may vary, but one thing is as predictable as clockwork about the mail: catalogs. They're pushed through—or jammed in—the hinged slot in my front door in multiples these days. (Apparently they refuse to travel alone.) And as the retail mania that accompanies each holiday season intensifies, the "thud" of them dropping into the hallway gets louder and more pronounced.

There's Horchow and Williams Sonoma and Sundance. Nordstrom and Crate and Barrel. Restoration Hardware and Levenger. Like pretty magazines you don't have to pay for, the catalogs are stuffed with color and craftsmanship and beautiful photography. Oh—and they're full of things I don't need but could be enticed to want if I lingered long enough over their pages.

I have to confess I have a favorite. It's Pottery Barn: fat and full of artfully arranged rooms and carefully collected accessories. It's not so lavish that it seems out of reach or so ordinary that it doesn't spark my imagination. And when the last one came, I figured out why it's so alluring: *It contains no people.* Not a single model breaks into the spaces of the Pottery Barn life, so it's easy to imagine that it could be *my* life.

That perfectly arranged table could be *my* tabletop. (Well, barring good judgment and a budget it could.) The sofa with a textured throw draped over the end and pillows off-handedly placed only needs *me* to curl up there with a steaming mug of tea. The pristine bathroom with not a single sign of toothpaste or damp towels is ready for me to stroll in and muss it up. And the plush, duvet covered bed shows no signs that anyone recently sat on the foot of it to put on shoes, then forgot to smooth it back.

The catalog life seems perfect because *no one lives there!*

But I don't want the catalog life. Not really. I want peopled, imperfect, intimate life. Life with some things missing and others out of place. Life with interruptions and joys and sorrows and spontaneous but less-than-artful celebrations. I'm not made for the sterile, catalog life. No one is. That's why those Pottery Barn pages are unpopulated.

These days I'm celebrating that God didn't send us a catalog showing us how perfect things are in heaven. He entered our world—our messy, people-strewn, noisy, dirty world—not just to tell us about *his* dwelling place but to show us how to live in ours. Because he's not selling anything. He came to give away all that he has.

> But we do see Him who has been made for a little while lower than the angels, namely, Jesus, because of the suffering of death crowned with glory and honor, that by the grace of God He might taste death for everyone.
>
> Hebrews 2:9

My passion for perfection renders enjoyment of the less-than-perfect impossible. What freedom the joyful surprise of a single, imperfect, Christ-infused moment brings! When will I learn that it is ardor—and not order—that moves my heart from criticism to worship?

About Those Expiration Dates . . .

*C*leaning out the pantry or the refrigerator reminds me that almost everything that is packaged carries an expiration date. They're kind of helpful, actually. If you can't remember when you bought the can of soup you're holding, you can check the expiration date. Or, if you think the half and half might be past its prime but would rather not inhale deeply to confirm that fact—the telltale date is there on the carton, right at the top. How very convenient!

One day as I straightened and reorganized my "perishables," it occurred to me that fresh produce doesn't have an expiration date . . . but one glance at a tomato can tell you if it's overripe. Bananas get spotted and turn brown. Lemons and limes become tough and harden. Even without a stamped code these are no-brainers. But faith is different. There are no coded dates or sure organic signs to help you know when yours is no longer fresh.

It takes more than a passing glance to see that your faith is getting stale. That your devotion has soured. That your passion for God's kingdom has dried and shriveled past the point of recognition. No series of etched or printed numbers can tell you that you're about to tap last month's obedience, or recycle last week's praise.

So if we're not paying attention, we can use what we shouldn't. And if we're not vigilant enough to routinely examine our own hearts, we can pass off a lot of second-rate stuff and call it "fresh."

God doesn't mean for us to hold on to yesterday's goods. He gave his people "groceries" in the wilderness, but the food was good only on the day it arrived. "Don't hoard it," he told them. "If you do, it will go bad." He wanted them to depend upon him, and see that his mercies really *were* new every morning, and that his faithfulness really was great.

Jesus suggested that his disciples should ask God for "daily bread," given "this day" and not weeks or months in advance, or in perpetuity. He wanted them to realize that the Bread of Life comes minute by minute, hour by hour, day by day.

Once the refrigerator and pantry are clean and straight, it's probably a good time to open wide the doors of my heart too and ask my Provider what's old and needs to go. I don't have to worry if the shelves look bare when he's done. He is the source of all that I need. There's more where this stuff came from. Plenty more.

> And my God will supply all your needs according to His riches in glory in Christ Jesus.
>
> Philipppians 4:19

How can you tell you're using "expired" faith? How do you know if your obedience is fresh and your praise is still near its prime? By this: how distant—in time or experienced presence—have you become from its source? Really? Isn't it time to draw near again?

Finding Feathers

One on the sidewalk as I walked the dog. One at the grocery store—right next to my car, driver's side. One standing upright in the grass at the park near my house. Even one in the garage (not a high bird-traffic area), near the washing machine. Lately I've been finding feathers. Nearly a dozen now—and not old, matted, musty ones. Perfect feathers . . .

blue, brown, white, and grey—that look as if their previous owners might have left them as a calling card.

Some people find pennies. I am finding feathers.

Here's the other coincidence (or not): on the oversized blackboard that covers one wall in my dining room, weeks ago I scrawled this snippet of an Emily Dickinson poem, and drew a few chalky feathers around it: "Hope is the thing with feathers/That perches in the soul,/And sings the tune—without the words,/And never stops at all."[1]

Now that I'm finding feathers, I'm thinking a lot more of hope. I'm thinking of it more and trying not to squelch it when I feel it rising in my heart. I'm forcing myself to watch my hometown baseball team roll into September, six games back in the wild card race and too far behind the Cardinals to care. Sometimes watching breaks my heart, but I'm not going to stop. Wilder things have happened. I can hope.

I'm hoping one day soon for a morning so cool that summer will retreat for the last time this year and leave the trees in my front yard no choice but to begin dropping their leafy confetti on fall's quiet parade.

I'm hoping older, deeper hopes too. Secret ones that just get richer with the years and never seem to fade. I'm finding feathers, and so I think, *Why not?*

It's not the feathers themselves. They're only a reminder. A handful of feathers don't hold much weight, literally or figuratively. But my hope is anchored elsewhere . . . anchored deep to something strong and unshakable. A friend of mine once said, "Choose hope. It's absolutely reasonable." She's not a kooky optimist, and neither am I. She's a follower of the One who *gave* hope its feathers and makes it sing. We know the Risen One. And because we know him, our hope is reasonable.

Not everyone's finding feathers. (I know. I asked a couple of friends, just to be sure.) Or maybe not everyone's noticing them. But I am. And I'm hopeful. Because the eternal, living object of my hope is dauntless, relentless, and wise. And because he pulled off the ultimate turnaround when he breathed life back into his dead Son, and into me.

Hope is *his* calling card. And I'm finding it everywhere.

> Now may the God of hope fill you with all joy and peace in believing, so that you will abound in hope by the power of the Holy Spirit.
>
> Romans 15:13

Feathers (or any other created thing) may be a reminder to me to hope—but my hope is validated by a single, historical event: the resurrection of Jesus Christ. Can you see what you hope for in light of that miracle and allow the God of hope to fill you with joy and peace now, today?

Finding (More) Feathers

I first wrote about finding feathers because for a few weeks one fall I was. Then the following spring, I began finding them not one at a time, but in scatterings of seven. I understand how odd this sounds. It *seemed* odd. (Someone will be moved to write and explain to me the molting patterns of birds—and while I wouldn't mind knowing, that's not the point at all.) The feathers reminded me of hope, thanks to the beautiful words of poet Emily Dickinson. And they came at a variety of times, in a variety of colors and sizes.

So, at the risk of being thought strange, consider with me what might be gleaned from a few unexplained feather-finding episodes.

Isn't it possible that God might choose to speak hope, or encouragement, or wonder or direction or reassurance *in any way he chooses, any time he chooses?* After all, he is still the God who crafted feathers, and lit up desert bushes, and caused a donkey to speak, and fire to fall, and fleece to be wet, then dry, and seas to part—isn't he? Sometimes he shouts. Sometimes he whispers. Sometimes he seems to wink, as if to say, "I'm here—and nothing slips my notice. No detail is unimportant, and I rule over everything that you see."

I'd be far, far too careless with the things of God if I told you I know for certain what the feathers mean. I don't. Maybe they're a whisper. Maybe they're a wink. Maybe, if I find still more of them, they'll add up to one big shout. Or maybe not. What I *am* sure of is this: God invades our world often. He invades *my* world often. And I'm afraid I miss too many of those moments because I'm simply not expecting them. I don't look for them. I don't listen, and watch, and hope to hear his voice in whatever way he chooses to speak. But when I found feathers, I began to pay closer attention.

I began to keep my eyes and ears open for him, and my heartstrings tuned. I longed to take in the small things, as well as the large ones, and to bless his name for every single wonder that I passed. And doing that caused me to glory in the reality of an awesome, mighty, all-knowing God who delights in delighting me with the littlest of things. I'm not still finding feathers. But I am still learning—finally learning—to feather my nest with his love.

> I wait for the LORD, my soul does wait, and in His word do I hope. My soul waits for the Lord more than the watchmen for the morning; indeed, more than the watchmen for the morning. O Israel, hope in the LORD; for with the LORD there is lovingkindness, and with Him is abundant redemption.
>
> Psalm 130:5–7

O, God of feathers and findings and whispered love, awaken my soul to your presence and tune my heart to sing your praise!

King of Hearts

What a fascinating, marvelous, miraculous creation is the heart! Its muscular right and left chambers continuously pump blood without reminder, as its various valves and vessels skillfully circulate that life-extending fluid. It works without assistance from us and even compensates as best it can for its own flaws. But although it has many parts, the heart functions as a whole, or not at all.

When things go wrong with our physical hearts, they must either be repaired or replaced. While some diseased or malfunctioning organs (like a spleen or an appendix) may simply be removed to affect healing, the heart must stay. And although other ailing parts may be cut away so that we make do with only a fraction of them, a man's heart cannot be divided and remain viable.

Years ago, working on the administrative staff of a large teaching hospital, I was afforded the opportunity to view open-heart surgery from the domed observatory over one busy operating suite. I will probably never do so again, but I am glad to have had that privileged perspective at least once.

What I learned from watching a heart repaired is this: heart surgery is messy; even brutal. And the human body really *is* fearfully and wonderfully made. Not only can it survive such a bloody, barbaric invasion of flesh and bone, it can actually be healed by it! Yet as amazing and intricate as a gifted surgeon's work on the human heart may appear,

God's work goes deeper still. The surgeon can locate damaged tissue or blocked vessels, but he cannot pinpoint the place in any heart that falls in love, or chooses sin, or cries out in fear, or longs to worship. Those places are hidden to him, but they are not hidden to God. He can touch them with laser-like accuracy and consummate skill.

Here's an even more amazing truth: my heart is not only God's creation, it is his permanent home. There is no part of it, no chamber, no valve, no muscle or memory or scar—that is unfamiliar to him. He rules the place. He ransomed it. It is his, and his alone. And when he wooed and won my heart once upon a time, he did not refurbish it, paint over it, or patch it. He came in and made it new. He is *still* renewing it, some thirty-five years later. I've been on the table that long. And his gentle invasion is—and has been—healing of the surest, sweetest kind to me.

We are so afraid to surrender to God our whole hearts. We'd rather rule our own flawed and pathetic little kingdoms than live as heirs in his. But halfhearted following is not following at all. Christ didn't come to die for half of your heart, or half of mine. He wants the whole thing, and by all rights he should have it. After all, he is the King of hearts.

> Moreover, I will give you a new heart and put a new spirit within you; and I will remove the heart of stone from your flesh and give you a heart of flesh. I will put My Spirit within you and cause you to walk in my My statutes . . . so you will be My people, and I will be your God.
>
> Ezekiel 36:26–28

Have you dissected your heart before God in a way that seeks to exclude him from some part of it, however small? Can you see the folly of that when you consider that he is the maker of it to begin with?

Bargain-Basement Deals

*H*ave you ever found a deal? I mean something that was marked so ridiculously low you felt as if buying it would be tantamount to stealing? My sister set a family shopping standard for deals when she bought an entire set of beautiful table linens for the price of a single *napkin*. No kidding. It was a deal.

I once bought an old copy of *Ben Hur* in a rolling cart of rejected books, then later that same week found the identical edition (a first!) in an antique bookseller's locked cabinet, tagged for $425. (I had paid $11.) I didn't make money on my literary deal, though. I'd already given the book away to a man I loved whose favorite story of all time was . . . *Ben Hur*. (I did, however, suggest to him that if he were ever tempted to sell the book in a garage sale he should call me first.)

Bargain-basement deals make for good stories. Who doesn't like to imagine gaining something of great worth with a less-than-great expenditure? Who wouldn't like to think they'd offered the lowest bid on a great house . . . and won? Or somehow beat a car salesman at his own game? Or found a once-grand treasure that was worth a mint, but, minus its original luster, was marked down to nothing?

Once, in a small village in Brazil, I asked a young woman who said she believed in God what it was that kept her from following him. She worked as a housekeeper in a large hospital in a nearby city. The main room of her home had a dirt floor and no running water. There was a roof over us, but we sat in well-worn, plastic lawn chairs. She looked at me as if the answer was obvious, and then said, her voice barely above a whisper, "Material things." I had thought she was impoverished. She felt well-off enough to be distracted by her possessions.

Most of the time, we're all about the deal. But I wonder if much of what we have didn't cost us too little, instead of too much.

I have friendships whose real value far exceeds the small-ish investment I've made in them. But that doesn't make me a relational "winner." It makes me the safe-but-sorry loser. And I still ache when I remember a desperate kid I poured a year of my life (and untold prayers and tears) into, with no apparent gain. I don't even know his where-abouts today, or if he is alive. But I count it one of the richest experiences of my life . . . and one I wouldn't trade, even for the ring I'd always hoped to wear on the third finger of my left hand.

So here's the bottom line: sometimes the true value is *in the spending*. And sometimes spending prodigiously for something the world holds cheap is not foolish but wise. Sometimes it's the things that cost us the most—not what we got for a song—that are most worth having. Or even losing.

Sometimes it's just not about the deal. It's about spending yourself right out of business.

Again, the kingdom of heaven is like a merchant seeking fine pearls, and upon finding one pearl of great value, he went and sold all that he had and bought it.

Matthew 13:45–46

Merchants buy and sell . . . and make a living doing so. For a merchant to sell his entire inventory for something he longed for and intended to keep was to essentially shut his operation down. Is there anything you desire so much that you'd spend yourself out of business to have it? There was for God. It was you.

Any Tree That Isn't Mine

I have a wish list, even though it isn't written down anywhere. I'll bet you do too. I don't know what's on your list, but I can quickly cite some of the bigger, recurring items on mine: A buttercream, VW Beetle with a black rag top. A good, godly husband and a family of my own. A horse . . . and a place to put it that doesn't violate municipal deed restrictions. And anything hanging in my closet with a size 8 tag that I could comfortably wear.

I saw the car on my list this week. I even parked next to it so that I could peek inside. And I've imagined that I glimpsed my husband more than once—although not recently. I finger the size 8's in stores from time to time, but even at my leanest—given the bone structure I inherited on my father's side of the family—it's not likely to happen. Each time I see something on my wish list, I feel my heart go out. There's an insistent little voice that says, "I still want that. Why hasn't God allowed me to have it?"

It's far, far too easy to consider the account of man's fall in the book of Genesis and imagine (go ahead and laugh) that if *I'd* been Eve, things might have happened differently. But let's face it: we all want the tree that isn't ours. *Any* tree that isn't ours.

There's no doubt in my mind that Eden was lush . . . beautiful . . . fragrant. I'm sure it was a treat for the senses and a deeply satisfying place to call home. But confronted with the one thing that was off-limits to her, Eve's satisfaction with Paradise wilted. Told that there was one tree that wasn't hers, she could think of little else. She wanted little else. All the goodness of the garden lost its shine when she remembered that single tree.

And most days, I'm no different.

But what if I saw those other "trees" as cues to offer thanks for all that *is* mine? What if every "Beetle sighting" was my cue to thank God for safe, reliable transportation—or that my car actually started up this morning when I got in and turned the key? What if dinner with married friends or a trip to Baby Gap for a shower gift reminded me to thank him that I'm not *unhappily* married and that there are children all around me who need extra love? What if a drive to the country in April didn't make me sigh deeply for the horse I don't have but made me grateful for the cute, apartment-sized dog draped over the back of my city-girl sofa? And what if a glance at a well-clad, gaunt mannequin reminded me that I'm clothed in righteousness and made me glad? Wouldn't that be a healthier approach?

There will always be a tree that isn't mine. But I'd be a fool to miss the forest that is, longing for it.

> I will give thanks to the LORD with all my heart; I will tell of all Your wonders. I will be glad and exult in You; I will sing praise to Your name, O Most High.
>
> Psalm 9:1–2

When do our longings go wrong? Is it in that moment when we allow desire to deaden satisfaction and then become resentment? Or is it the moment we stop wanting God more than anything else, trusting that he knows what's best for us? Elisabeth Elliot once said, "God is God. I dethrone Him in my heart when I demand that He act in ways that satisfy my idea of justice."

Missing Pieces

An old chandelier that I could not ignore sat in my attic for three years. It originally hung in the upstairs bedroom of the nearly seventy-year-old duplex where I live—but I had pictured it downstairs (in my "half") since I first laid eyes on it. I imagined it in the entry hall, but it would have hung too low and caught the front door each time I opened it. Then I thought the bathroom might be a fun spot—but there it would have overpowered the tiny room. I considered the study too, except it already has a ceiling fan—nice in summer when the midday sun warms up the windows and the room as well.

When my landlord came around to repair some tiny cracks in the dining room ceiling, I asked him to consider replacing the light in *that* room with the old chandelier that was gathering dust. He agreed and brought it down. The chandelier had five delicate, etched glass globes, and all of them were intact. From the base of each globe hung five glass "bobs," each about four inches long. Every one was identical: a round "eye" connected to a triangular "stem," and tapering to a six-sided point that looked like an arrowhead. One edge of the stem was cut like a key in a curved and jagged pattern.

It was only after I had looked at it for a while that I realized the center of the fixture was missing pieces. A section of glass that looked like an inverted buttercup should have had one of the same five "bobs" hanging on each petal. Instead it had none. I asked my landlord to hang it anyway—at least there was symmetry in what was missing. I figured the absent pieces would be impossible to replace and decided the chandelier's charm was only slightly diminished by their absence.

A short time later I stopped by a place that houses "architectural antiques"—old doors, windows, doorknobs, scrollwork, and fixtures—plus a lot of what could only be called junk. On one counter I found a tray of cut glass teardrops that looked like they belonged to a light fixture. "Do you have any more of these?" I asked the fellow minding the store. "Yep," he said, and led me to a bin that was full of chandelier castoffs. "Fish around," he suggested. So I did.

And one by one, out of the hundreds of pieces of glass in the bin, I pulled five that would fit my salvaged chandelier. They were exactly like the ones already on it—right down to the jagged edge of the stem, and they made the fixture complete again for less than $10.

"So what?" you may wonder. So this: we might *think* we're complete enough, whole enough, just the way we are. But "complete enough" is not complete. And "whole enough" is not whole. God has resources we know nothing about, and he is able to replace our missing pieces. Not with "make-do" stuff—but with the stuff that was meant to be ours all along. He's just that good at restoration.

O God, restore us and cause Your face to shine upon us, and we will be saved.

Psalm 80:3

"We're half-hearted creatures," said C. S. Lewis, and "far, far too easily pleased." Like the Israelites who settled comfortably outside of Canaan, we convince ourselves that "better" is good enough because we can't imagine best. What is missing in you that only God can replace? What has fallen into ruin that only he can restore? Dare to imagine his best for you.

The One-Eyed Tiger

*H*ave you ever had the sense that—quite without trying—you've stumbled onto something truly wondrous? Maybe you'd vaguely enjoyed a particular author's style, his insights, his characters . . . then suddenly you turn a page and it hits you: *This is what he's been setting me up for all along. This is the reason he bothers to write at all.*

I had that feeling the first time I saw the one-eyed tiger.

My friend Karelyn is the tiger's creator. She is an artist. A painter. I've seen a fair amount of her work and found something to appreciate in all of it. She is quite good. But when my gaze fell on the one-eyed tiger, I was hooked— and I understood at that moment that my heart was seeing far more than my eyes could actually take in.

"My One-Eyed Tiger, 1996," the painting's notation read. *"Oil on canvas, 36 x 48 in."* It was a still life and (she explained later to me) something of a study in textures. Two swathes of fabric—one wool and one velvet—lie draped over a dark leather chair. In the chair is an odd trio of objects. A round, wooden canister with silver trim. A translucent crystal goblet. And between them, a battered, stuffed tiger with a jaunty orange bow around its neck . . . clearly missing its left eye.

My words don't do it justice. You'd have to see it, I think, to be caught by its spell. I once saw the "real" tiger, removed from the context of the painting and tossed atop an armoire in Karelyn's apartment, but the effect was altogether different. It was like seeing an old friend in a place you didn't expect him to be. He looked odd there . . . and lost. But in her painting, settled amongst fine wood and leather and crystal and wool, he looked at home. Well worn, but fearless. Wrecked, but in his rightful place. Weathered, but quietly regal.

Because I know my friend's story, I could guess that the one-eyed tiger is more for her than a study in contrasting textures. But art of any kind is not simply what it means to the artist—it's what it means to those who experience it too. Karelyn's story is not my story, yet in my heart, I think I know exactly how it feels to be a one-eyed tiger.

Today, the painting I loved at first sight hangs in my home. I didn't purchase it. (I couldn't afford it then—and it is still not in my budget.) Instead it came to me the way so many treasured things come: as a gift I didn't ask for, and cannot repay. Each time I see it, it brings a lump to my throat, and a quiet surge of joy to my heart. And it does something else to me that few things do: it leaves me feeling clumsy with words. So I'll let someone else speak what I struggle to articulate, and maybe you will understand:

> But we have this treasure in earthen vessels, so that the surpassing greatness of the power will be of God and not from ourselves; we are afflicted in every way, but not crushed; perplexed, but not despairing; persecuted, but not forsaken; struck down, but not destroyed; always carrying about in the body the dying of Jesus, so that the life of Jesus also may be manifested in our body.
>
> 2 Corinthians 4:7–10

Life and grace and peace to you today, from the one-eyed tiger and from me.

God's "iPod-ness"

I had watched the "shadow guy" gyrate to U2's *Vertigo* for over a year without one twinge of desire. I had nodded politely at friends' enthusiastic demos of their own multi-megabyte, palm-size music libraries and not felt a whit of envy. But when my teenaged niece got an iPod Shuffle for her birthday, I felt myself begin to waver.

"Look, Aunt Leigh," she said as she showed me her traveling song collection—no bigger than a pack of gum. "How cool is *this*?" Then she pressed it twice and handed it over, and when I put the tiny sound bits in my ear, I heard Josh Groban as if he was in my living room. As with almost every piece of personal technology invented, the iPod had become smaller, cheaper, and a lot less complicated.

The demo did its magic. I ordered one for myself less than a month later, and even for the hardware-challenged, found it less than daunting to configure. I was afraid I would have to call the aforementioned niece for assistance, but I didn't. I confess I was so proud that I sent her a giddy email saying I had managed to load a hundred or so songs "all by myself." The message line on her return email said simply, "iPod-ness."

I liked that.

I decided, "iPod-ness" was an ever-changing, randomly ordered, and finite subset of the words and melodies I love best. A sample, if you will, of a much bigger library of music that is far too vast to comfortably contain or transport. Of all the songs in the world ever composed and sung, my iPod holds less than a sliver. So what's that got to do with God? Maybe this: I don't believe I've seen or heard even a little of what he's been pouring forth since time began. I'm pretty sure that the Grand Canyon—magnificent as it is—*isn't* his defining work. That crafting butterflies and wheat fields and a baby's sigh didn't begin to exhaust his creativity. That all the randomly ordered samplings I've seen of his goodness and his grace *put together* wouldn't crowd his iPod, if he had one.

There's more to him than I can see or know or comprehend. God's "iPod-ness" is the understanding that I know only in part what I will one day (praise him!) know in full. That I can't imagine the fullness of his mercy and love and grace. Yes, I know Jesus—and believe that all the fullness of deity dwells in him. But it will take more than the lifetime I have here to take him in.

Wouldn't it be a shame to be satisfied with only a shuffled sample of what I think are his "greatest hits," marvelous as they are? God's "iPod-ness" reminds me that there's infinitely more of him than I can carry in my pocket. And I'm so very glad that's true.

> And there are also many other things which Jesus did, which, if they were written in detail, I suppose that even the world itself could not contain the books that would be written.
>
> John 21:25

J. B. Phillips wrote a tiny Christian classic entitled simply Your God is Too Small. *He saw what I'm only just beginning to grasp: my attempts to make God "portable" in no way downsize his true nature and character. I'm diminished by that exercise—but he is not.*

137

Respecting the Storm

For several weeks my hometown was "operation central" for victims of a storm called Katrina. Thousands of evacuees from Louisiana and Mississippi came for refuge. Many lost all that they had and looked to build new lives here, or ultimately elsewhere. It was a serious storm, Katrina. And serious storms have serious and deadly consequences.

Soon after Katrina hit, another storm gathered steam seven hundred miles from the Texas coast, and in context, no one made light of it. Local residents stripped store shelves of bottled water and batteries. Meteorologists went into commando mode. They named the new storm Rita—and from the very beginning she got respect, because we'd already seen the devastation that category 4 winds and rising water can produce.

Isn't that just like us? We're such "show me" people. We place great confidence in our own invincibility, and in the resources we've amassed to make ourselves safe and comfortable. We put our faith in windows and walls and wheels . . . in ATM's and gasoline pumps and groceries. And until those things prove vulnerable, we keep on believing we're beyond the threat of other forces.

It takes wicked storms like Katrina and Rita to teach us to respect what newscasters call "the power of nature." We learn to respect the storm when we see the undeniable evidence of its power. Even so, I wonder how many *still* deny the power of the storm *maker*? Physical lives can be rebuilt. I've seen evidence of it time and time again. But spiritual lives must be rebirthed. We deny at our own peril the presence and power of the God who rides above the wind. He may look harmless and detached, but he is not. He may seem removed from our insulated, day-to-day existence, but he is not. We may question whether or not he cares for us or sees our plight, but that question was answered once for all with the terrible death and glorious resurrection of his only Son.

His ways are beyond our scrutiny and far, far above our understanding. We are not as independent as we pretend. We need him more—much more—than we let on. And if we think that we will somehow stand against the winds of sin and the floodwaters of judgment without him, then we've simply failed to show him the fear, awe, and respect that he is due.

Storms—physical ones—teach a lesson about greater, invisible things. We are small and weak and lost and hopeless, no matter how well protected we feel. And the only sure way to safety is to respect the One who commands every storm, trusting him to deliver us from what we cannot hope to conquer on our own.

> When my life was ebbing away, I remembered you, LORD, and my prayer rose to you, to your holy temple. Those who cling to worthless idols forfeit the grace that could be theirs. But I, with a song of thanksgiving, will sacrifice to you.
>
> Jonah 2:7–9 NIV

It chills me to think of how much grace I have forfeited in my life because I believed I did not need it. It humbles me to consider how much grace I have received only because I saw my need and asked it from the One who could supply.

Considering Monovision

$\mathcal{M}$y eyes haven't been working so well. For months I've struggled to read small print with my contact lenses in and not had much success. I used to laugh as my non-lens-wearing friends adjusted the distance between their eyes and menus or instruction manuals, or peered over the tops of their glasses to see. I may have smugly thought myself impervious to the little indignities of age—but let the record show that I am not.

My optometrist kindly offered a suggestion that has spared me reading glasses and so far seems to be working well. He called it monovision: strengthening one lens and weakening another, or, in my case, abandoning one altogether. The result? One eye "learns" it's the "distance" eye, and the other picks up the nearsighted duties. They compensate for and cooperate with each other, calling dominance over the task at hand the way a second baseman and a center fielder might negotiate a mid-range pop fly. ("Got it! Mine!")

Somehow, without my brain engaging, my eyes do their adjusting and focus appropriately. If only my heart would learn to do the same.

Lately I've been focusing on what isn't. What I don't have and others do. What isn't in my portfolio or my living room, or my name. Who isn't in my corner or on my side. As you might expect, my perception has become distorted. I am not easily discerning the fine print of happiness. I no longer recognize beauty or abundance up close—only at a distance, in someone else's hands.

I'm not sure when this happened, any more than I'm sure of when my eyes could no longer manage small fonts well. One day I just knew. Instead of looking at the goodness in my life, I had focused in like a laser on my own lack. Instead of looking with gratefulness at the past and learning from it, I was gazing at the future with fear. But Jesus said that kind of focus was wrong. That it would get me nowhere, fast.

> I tell you not to worry about your life. Don't worry about having something to eat, drink, or wear. Isn't life more than food or clothing? Look at the birds in the sky! They don't plant or harvest. They don't even store grain in barns. Yet your Father in heaven takes care of them. Aren't you worth more than birds? Can worry make you live longer? Why worry about clothes? Look how the wild flowers grow. They don't work hard to make their clothes. But I tell you that Solomon with all his wealth wasn't as well clothed as one of them. God gives such beauty to everything that grows in the fields, even though it is here today and thrown into a fire tomorrow. He will surely do even more for you! Why do you have such little faith?
>
> Matthew 6:25–30, CEV

Jesus told his followers to look at the birds. Really look. To focus on them, see and consider. Then he suggested they let their gaze linger on the wildflowers too and understand that even though these buds were small and transient, they were deeply valued and exquisitely made. Birds and flowers don't manufacture a thing, and yet they always seem to have enough. Do you *see* them? Do I?

My eyes are adjusting to the realities of a new season. And to those realities that remain season-less. I'm struggling less and considering more. I know it's about time.

> You open Your hand and satisfy the desire of every living thing.
>
> Psalm 145:16 NKJV

*When my grasping heart feels lack, I see lack. But when
my grateful heart senses plenty, I see resources I had never
noticed before. Do you have monovision? Should you have
it checked, perhaps?*

No Hope—or New Hope?

*M*y favorite form of exercise is a brisk early morning walk through my neighborhood—sometimes before the
sun comes up. I walk east so that I can watch the horizon go
from dark to light in colors nearly impossible to describe,
and I almost always see something new.

On a heavy-garbage pickup day, I spotted something
abandoned on the curb of a favorite tree-lined street. As
I got closer I could see that it was an exercise machine—
left lying on its side like a capsized metal cricket, waiting
for the trashmen to rumble down the block and toss it in
their truck.

I suppose it's not terribly unusual to abandon an exercise machine, or an exercise program. I've abandoned a
few in my time. But in January (and it was) most of us are
purchasing such machines or beginning such programs,
not leaving them behind. In January, most of us still have
hope in our resourcefulness, our own determination, our
own power to move mountains—even if the mountain is
us! In January we're optimistic that we have just the right
mind-set to achieve our targeted goals, regardless of past
failures. So why did my neighbor leave his exerciser on the
curb two weeks into a brand-new year?

As I walked, I imagined all kinds of scenarios. Maybe
he bought the machine *last* January, and it hadn't had the
hoped-for results—or it had, and he was done with all the

effort. (Big mistake.) Maybe he'd begun another program or acquired a better machine. Or maybe he overestimated his own dedication and simply failed to follow through.

The abandoned machine pointed to one of two things: either its former owner had no hope, or he had a new hope.

In Christ we aren't just given a mulligan—we're given new hope. We can begin again—it's true. But we no longer hope in our own goodness, or in God's willingness to overlook our shortcomings, or judge us favorably in light of someone else whose performance we deem even less worthy than our own. We don't hope in our own power to effect change, or to manage the circumstances of our lives. Instead we have a new and living hope: we have a Savior who defeated death itself, and who lives to tell.

This new hope of ours is attached to something solid, immovable, and certain. It's an anchor, this hope. And its heavy end rests in a place where we've never been before but one day will.

They say the road to hell is paved with good intentions. I'm beginning to wonder if the road to heaven isn't littered with abandoned ones: left-behind intentions that, like the exerciser a few blocks over, might just be a sign that a new and better hope has taken up residence.

> Blessed be the God and Father of our Lord Jesus Christ, who according to His great mercy has caused us to be born again to a living hope through the resurrection of Jesus Christ from the dead.
>
> 1 Peter 1:3

> This hope we have as an anchor of the soul, a hope both sure and steadfast and one which enters within the veil, where Jesus has entered as a forerunner for us.
>
> Hebrews 6:19–20

Paradox is the hallmark of the kingdom of heaven. I can almost count on the truth of God's kingdom being counterintuitive to my own way of thinking. Who'd imagine that hopelessness is the very door to hope? That failure is the forerunner of glory? That when a seed falls to the earth and dies, something impossible becomes possible, and life takes root and grows?

Loving the Weight of the Wood

*H*oly week—the days leading to the celebration of our Lord's resurrection—always leaves me thinking more than I normally do about the cross. Maybe it's the movies: *The Robe, Ben-Hur,* and now, *The Passion of the Christ.* They draw me not to studies of redemption, propitiation, expiation, or sacrifice. They draw me to reflect. Not on the eternal and obvious *meaning* of the cross but to its actual timber and its awful weight. And the image that remains fixed in my mind—particularly from *The Passion*'s stunning array of imagery—is this one: my Lord Jesus carrying the cross. His cross. For a good distance he bore it alone, and then with the help of a passerby whose name we're told was Simon of Cyrene.

Both men struggled under its weight, but it was Jesus who seemed to embrace it like a lover, even as he stumbled, staggered, and fell beneath it. It was Jesus whose hands both clutched and caressed it, and whose face was pressed against it in agony and in desperate ardor. It was my Jesus who loved the weight of the wood he carried for me.

If I could, I would only meditate on this, offer thanks for this, and wonder at it. But because I am his, more is asked of me. He invites me not just to consider this—but to imitate it. To somehow love the scene and the means of my own large and small sacrifices, day by day. He said, "If anyone wishes to come after Me, he must deny himself, and take up his cross daily and follow Me" (Luke 9:23). He said, "And he who does not take his cross and follow after Me is not worthy of Me" (Matt. 11:38).

My confession is this. My imitation of my Savior is too often shabby. Weak. If I somehow manage, on a good day, to take up my cross and get my shoulder beneath it, I am likely to be found complaining about its roughness, or railing about its weight, or resisting its encumbrance. I don't love the weight of the wood so much.

But we're only human, right? And rough beams like cancer and widowhood and loneliness and betrayal are almost impossible to embrace, aren't they? Aren't prodigal children and infertility and unemployment decidedly unlovely and unlovable? Isn't regret repulsive and heartbreak hopeless? They would be, except for this. The cross of Christ was the doorway to the resurrection. The ugly tool of Roman execution was the means by which God's very Son would show his Father's glorious plan. He loved the weight of the wood because he knew how the story would end. And he wanted nothing else more than the privilege of playing his part.

> Then they compelled a certain man, Simon a Cyrenian, the father of Alexander and Rufus, as he was coming out of the country and passing by, to bear His cross. And they brought Him to the place Golgotha, which is translated, Place of a Skull. Then they gave Him wine mingled with myrrh to drink, but He did not take it. And when they crucified Him, they divided His garments, casting lots for them to determine what every man should take. Now it was the third hour, and they crucified Him.
>
> Mark 15:21–25 NKJV

145

I love his cross. I do. I just don't always love to imitate him in carrying mine. I don't always love the weight of the wood, but Jesus loved it well.

Ordinary
Moments

Changing the Porch Light

Although I have an upstairs neighbor that shares a porch with me, not once has she changed our porch light. Ever. She uses it of course. She turns it off and on. But when my neighbor notices (as she must) that the lightbulb over the front door has burned out, she simply waits as long as it takes for me to change it.

She's not physically challenged in any way. She's probably a decade younger than me. She waters her plants. Walks her dog. Even feeds the large and growing stray cat in our neighborhood that mistakenly thinks its address is the same as mine. But she doesn't do porch lights. I know, because I've tried to wait her out.

The longest I've gone is a week—and it's pointless, really. Because all that happens is I fumble in the dark for my keys when I come home late and get madder and madder as each day goes by that I have to be the one to do the chore.

It's not the money. Lightbulbs, relatively speaking, are cheap. It's the principle of the thing. At least that's what I keep telling myself. Still, when the porch light burns out and it becomes clear that once again she has no intention of changing the bulb, I abandon my principles and do it anyway.

I climb up on a footstool underneath the awning, coax the crooked pin out of the bottom of the light fixture, and ease it open. Flakes of stuff that I'm certain were once flying insects fall into my upturned face, and I reach my hand in (past more flakes) to unscrew the burned-out bulb. Then I place it between my knees or in the pocket of my jeans, remove the new bulb from another pocket, and complete the annoying bit of maintenance.

All told it probably takes less than three minutes, start to finish. So why does it irritate me every time? Because I don't think it should be my job. Because I'm tired of being the one to do it. Because I think *she* should change at least every third or fourth bulb. And because every time I feel indignant pride rising up in me over something as silly as a lightbulb, I see how far I am from where I really want to be.

> Don't push your way to the front; don't sweet-talk your way to the top. Put yourself aside, and help others get ahead. Don't be obsessed with getting your own advantage. Forget yourselves long enough to lend a helping hand. Think of yourselves the way Christ Jesus thought of himself. He had equal status with God but didn't think so much of himself that he had to cling to the advantages of that status no matter what. . . . When the time came . . . he . . . took on the status of a slave. . . . He didn't claim special privileges. Instead, he lived a selfless, obedient life and then died a selfless, obedient death.
>
> Philippians 2:3–8 Message

So excuse me while I change the front porch lightbulb again. I've waited more than long enough.

I'm more vigilant about my rights than I am about "human rights." My pride asserts itself every time I do something I feel I shouldn't have to do. I'm all about justice, until I need mercy. How about you?

Caught!

I'm not usually caught, are you? Usually I have the reasoning power, the resources, the connections, and creativity it takes to work my way out of whatever difficult spot I might be in. Usually.

But lately I've found myself caught—and when I am truly caught, it's almost always by what I cannot change. I can't change another's heart or mind or past. I can't change illness or the economy or the fact that I'm single and childless and never planned to be either—at least not for this long. I can't even change who my heart goes out to. I can only choose whether or not I will be truthful to its sometimes awkward and inconvenient leanings. These are the places where I am caught.

But caught isn't necessarily the worst place for me to be. Caught, I am slower to act, more prone to ponder, more aware of others, and less sure of myself. Caught, I am a thousand times more likely to fall on my knees in desperate pleading.

Are you caught? In a marriage that isn't working anymore? In a lie that no one's discovered yet? In a heartbreak that stays fresh, even as its genesis grows more distant? In a sickness that a pill won't fix? A rift that words alone won't mend? Welcome to the odd company of the caught ones.

Paul said he was caught by a "thorn in the flesh"—an ailment of some sort that he called "a messenger of Satan to torment me—to keep me from exalting myself" (2 Cor. 12:7). He asked for God to take the thorn away. Who wouldn't? But God did not. Not the first time, or the second, or the third. So Paul, being caught, made friends with his captor. He heard God's answer: "My grace is enough; it's all you need. My strength comes into its own in your weakness" (2 Cor. 12:9 Message).

Caught, Paul began to look at the thing he could not change in a new way: "I quit focusing on the handicap and began appreciating the gift. It was a case of Christ's strength moving in on my weakness. Now I take limitations in stride, and with good cheer, these limitations that cut me down to size—abuse, accidents, opposition, bad breaks. I just let Christ take over! And so the weaker I get, the stronger I become" (2 Cor. 12:9–10 Message).

I'm rather new at being caught and not so graceful as Paul with it. I'd welcome change instead, but in a very few critical places I am held fast. He's not budging—and I can't move him. I'm caught, but I can testify to this: I'm holding on to see his strength and praying for his glory. I want him to put my fears to shame and bring me to the day when I can point to what he's done and say, "Look at him—isn't he good? Isn't my God good?"

You watch. You'll see. Till then, be caught with me.

For we rejoice when we ourselves are weak but you are strong; this we also pray for, that you be made complete.

2 Corinthians 13:9

Is there an area in which you too are caught? Could you come to say along with Paul that the weaker you get, the stronger you become?

Shine

When I was ten or eleven, I participated in a city-wide championship spelling bee. The "bee" contestants were all winners from their schools or school districts, and it's been quite a long time since, but I think there must have been one hundred or so of us in the competition. That's the truth of the story. I spelled a bunch of hard words in a row and got to go to a big meet. (Once a word-nerd, always a word-nerd.)

Now for the humbling footnote: I missed the very first word I was asked to spell, and it was only five letters long. I could have spelled "xylophone" or "prestidigitator"—but they didn't ask me to spell those words. They asked me to spell "easel." And I did: e-a-s-l-e. At the time I was also taking art lessons and painting on an e-a-s-e-l once a week. The judge leaned into her microphone and said a crisp, "That is incorrect." I went to my seat duly embarrassed. Five letters! Sheesh.

I'd mostly forgotten about my spelling bee bust until I saw a movie called *Akeelah and the Bee*. Maybe you heard about it in your local Starbucks, where it scored a major marketing coup. Its young protagonist Akeelah was something of a word-nerd too—although a much better speller than me. But she almost didn't compete in the bee because she was afraid of being different. Of being really good at something and standing out from her peers because of it.

To coax the competitor out of her, Akeelah's coach insisted that her deepest fear wasn't of inadequacy but of power. That she was a child of God who could not serve the world by playing it "small." He urged her to manifest the glory of God within, and to *shine*, giving no foothold to self-consciousness or self-doubt. Akeelah didn't make her gift. God gave it. And by using it, she only made his glory more evident.

Me, I'm a little shy. Maybe you are too. I don't like to do things that call too much attention to myself. I don't want anyone to examine me too closely. I know it's only a matter of time before I'll stumble and maybe miss a five-letter word. But even so, God has placed his Spirit within me and he asks me to shine. Not for my glory. For his.

Isn't it about time for us to swallow our fears and simply shine?

You are the light of the world. A city set on a hill cannot be hidden. Nor does anyone light a lamp and put it in a basket, but on the lampstand, and it gives light to all who are in the house. Let your light shine before men in such a way that they may see your good works, and glorify your Father who is in heaven.

Matthew 5:14–16

I've hidden my stuff under plenty of bushels and spent half my life hoping I'd blend in somehow. I never quite did. These days I hope to shine, because it's not about me and it never was. It's all about my God and how very good he is. He doesn't ask me if I mind being light. He tells me that I already am. I just need to do what light does. It shines.

Lost Ticket

*Y*ears ago living, breathing attendants in the dozen or so garages of my city's enormous medical center were replaced with an inhuman ticketing/pay kiosk system that—even though I worked there for nearly three years—still remains something of a mystery to me. It's supposed to work like this: you approach the garage entry (hopefully the one closest to the institution you are visiting!), push a button, and receive a ticket with a magnetic strip on it. The entry arm to said garage lifts to admit you. If you're lucky you find a parking space in this same garage (Not always, but that's another tale, for another day.) Then . . . and this is very important . . . you take your ticket with you after you've parked and guard it as if it were gold.

On this particular visit, I'm sure I carried mine into the hospital—but only one of us made it out. I tried walking over to the garage entry and pushing the button for another ticket, but the brain in the ticket-dispensing device must have detected that I wasn't a car and refused to comply.

So, with no attendant to tell my story to, I searched the face of the pay kiosk and pressed a fat button labeled "Call for assistance." After a few seconds a scratchy, female voice responded. I explained that I'd lost my ticket; she squawked back something about $10 and said, "Wait there for an attendant." How would he/she be arriving? When might I expect him or her? I didn't know. So I leaned up against the nearest wall to wait.

Within a minute, a man in scrubs arrived to pay his own way out of the garage. He saw me lingering near the kiosk with my hands in my pockets and asked if I was in line ahead of him to pay. "No," I told him, "I seem to have lost my ticket—so I'm waiting for someone to come and spring me." We exchanged a few other pleasantries, he paid the machine, then he stood for a while fumbling in his wallet. After a few seconds he produced a light green ticket, the same size as the white one I'd lost.

"I work here," he said, "and they give us a few 'get out of jail free' cards. I still have one left. When the attendant comes, he'll give you a 'lost ticket,' then you can feed this one in right after it. It's worth $10." Then he paused and smiled at me. "I was saving it for a rainy day," he said.

"Is it raining?" I asked him. He nodded his head yes. It was clear as a bell outside.

Then something even odder happened. After the attendant finally came and my green card had sprung me and zeroed out my balance, I drove to the garage exit, and before I could put in my proof of payment, *the barrier arm lifted.* Just like that. As I drove home I thought about what had just happened. I'd lost something I had to have. I had tried to remedy the situation myself by "working" the system already in place. No deal. Then a stranger came along and freely gave me what I needed at absolutely no cost to me . . . and by no merit of my own. And finally, just so I could see the exclamation point on the deal, the garage "god" recognized my justified status and let me go: guilty and freed not once but twice.

Great reminder. (And it still hadn't rained a drop.)

> For by grace you have been saved through faith; and that not of yourselves, it is the gift of God; not as a result of works, that no one may boast.
>
> Ephesians 2:8–9

My self-styled attempts at justification never seem to work. Do yours? No matter how well I plan, I simply cannot pay for my own mistakes. It's good for me to be reminded that God has another remedy.

Extra-Inning Exhaustion

I've been a baseball girl for a long time—beginning with the summer I spent scoring Little League contests for $5 a game and a sno-cone—and in my experience, nothing beats October baseball. In October, everything counts. And not just a little. A lot. In October, inches can mean the difference between going home and going on, and one pitch can quite literally change the course of an entire season. Tom Hanks said in *A League of Their Own*, "There is no crying in baseball," but he was bluffing. It's a game of tears, whether they're shed in full view, or not.

One fine weekend in October my hometown team survived the longest play-off game in the history of baseball: eighteen innings, five hours and fifty minutes. All but two players on the roster made it into the game. Only three ended it in their starting position. The worst thing about

155

the incredible marathon was that someone had to lose. The best thing was that it wasn't us.

When the game-ending home run sailed into the short porch in left field, adrenaline gave the guys in the dugout the fuel to leap the rail and pile into a riotous home plate happy dance. Because adrenaline was all they had left. Extra innings are exhausting—especially nine of them! But with no reserves remaining and everything on the line, quitting was absolutely out of the question.

Sometimes life demands extra innings. Sometimes we find ourselves on the field and locked in battle far longer than we imagined we could possibly go. But when the stakes are high, surrender is not an option. Bat-by-bat, out-by-out, inning-by-inning, we keep on. And as we do, character is formed. My granddad used to say, "It's a tough life if you don't weaken and die." Given that option, tough life is most assuredly the preferred choice.

I don't doubt my National League Division Series championship team woke up sore on Monday morning—especially the ones who are my contemporaries in age. But I can almost guarantee that they slept well on Sunday night. Because extra innings are the stuff of soul-satisfying slumber. Especially when you live again to play another day.

> For I consider that the sufferings of this present time are not worthy to be compared with the glory that is to be revealed to us. For the anxious longing of the creation waits eagerly for the revealing of the sons of God. For the creation was subjected to futility, not willingly, but because of Him who subjected it, in hope that the creation itself also will be set free from its slavery to corruption into the freedom of the glory of the children of God. . . . For in hope we have been saved, but hope that is seen is not hope; for who hopes for what he already sees? But if we hope for what we do not see, with perseverance we wait eagerly for it.

No one longs to be tested to their imagined limits and beyond. But when we are, we discover things about ourselves—and our God—that we might never know otherwise. If you're in extra innings today, thank God for the lessons you are sure to learn. He aims for you to be victorious and is not afraid for you to be spent.

Where's Your Treasure?

I've heard of people keeping their money in a mattress. One of my grandmothers even had a mayonnaise jar full of cash in her top dresser drawer. But I once saw the oddest "banking" arrangement that I've ever imagined. At a stoplight on a busy city street, I watched a shabbily dressed, dirty guy reach into a neatly trimmed hedge at McDonald's, pull out a blue plastic cup, and remove from it a wad of bills. He counted out four and replaced the cup in the same spot in which he'd found it.

As the light changed and I drove past, I tried to guess how the "system" worked. Did other people know about the blue cup bank, or was it this man's own private account? Did he make deposits too and then later return for withdrawals, or did someone else keep the kitty filled for him? Was it a give-what-you-can, take-what-you-need arrangement? Then my last thought was more pragmatic: *Is that secure?*

I mean, anyone could have taken his savings if they had known the bush to look under, right? How safe could a cup of money be near a fast-food stop at a high-traffic intersection? I wondered if the man I'd seen slept nearby, or if he visited the hedge often to make sure his investment was safe. I would have.

That's because we don't stray far from our treasure. We want to be sure of it. We keep returning to it for reassurance and security. We need to be certain of our treasure's whereabouts and to keep tabs on its availability. But here's the thing: no treasure is safe unless it exists within us or resides beyond us. Whether it's in a safe deposit box or an IRA, a hedge fund or a trust fund, real estate or art—it's vulnerable. Just as vulnerable, really, as if it were stashed in a blue plastic cup. Because the only stuff that lasts is the stuff you *can't* lock away.

The man I saw who made the "hedge fund" withdrawal probably wouldn't have been surprised if he had returned to find his account emptied. I'm sure he realized the risk of keeping his investment in an unguarded ring of foliage. But I probably put more faith than I should in my own "protected" assets . . . and check them more often than I need to.

The place that preoccupies my heart is the place where my treasure resides. The question is, what treasure? Where? And can I count on it to last?

> Do not store up for yourselves treasures on earth, where moth and rust destroy, and where thieves break in and steal. But store up for yourselves treasures in heaven, where moth and rust do not destroy, and where thieves do not break in and steal. For where your treasure is, there your heart will be also.
>
> Matthew 6:19–21 NIV

Is your stuff safe? That depends on where it is stored. And wherever that is, remember—your heart is kept in that same place.

Dinner for Two (Plus Two)

Sometimes no matter what you've planned, your plans are changed. I had invited a young friend over for a casual supper. My plan was to serve something simple so that I might focus my attention on her and on a topic we'd agreed ahead of time we would explore together.

Earlier in the day another friend had called and left a message: would I be agreeable to keeping her adorable six-month-old son while she and her husband took clients to a baseball game? Since friend one is young and flexible I thought one sleeping baby wouldn't alter our plans much. (I did say this baby is adorable, right? He is.)

Friend number two and I played telephone tag all day. The last message I left said simply, "Sure, bring him over on your way to the game if you like. I'll have a friend here, but it won't be a problem." When I didn't hear from her again, I forgot the matter entirely.

At around 6:00 p.m. (*friend one is early*, I thought) I opened the door to friend two, with a sleeping baby. When she saw the look on my face, she said, "You didn't get my last message, did you?" I didn't, but it didn't matter. Dinner was cooking nicely, the table was set, and everything seemed under control. I assured her it was fine and shooed her off to the park with confidence.

Friend one arrived on time; I announced that a six-month-old would be joining us, and as I expected, she gamely took it in stride. (It helped that she thought he was as cute as I did.) He began to fuss a little as I finished cooking, so I served dinner with him on my hip, then set him in his carrier seat on top of the dining room table. We finished our meal without much commotion, I did a quick diaper change (not on the table of course), then settled into the living room for conversation and dessert.

That's when the real fun started. My *own* baby—a spoiled prima donna of a dog—wasn't thrilled with the extra guest and the attention everyone but he was receiving. In a span of a few minutes, he had eaten my cup of fresh berries when I turned away (and licked the spoon), climbed on top of the dining room table and lapped butter from a dish, and, in an ultimate act of defiance, marched into my older guest's sight line and deliberately abandoned every rule he knows about housebreaking!

If I ever had any illusions about being the perfect hostess and having it all together, it took less than ten minutes to shatter them.

The next day, I received a voice mail from the sweet friend who had witnessed the three-ring circus in my living room, and this is what she said: "I'm still laughing, and I want you to know that that might be the most fun I've ever had with you."

Her words were a lesson to me: intimacy is not about how smoothly you perform. It's about what happens when plans change—and how willing you are to appear in your own production as the less-than-perfect specimen that you are.

(I think God must have laughed too.)

"For where two or three have gathered together in My name, I am there in their midst."

Matthew 18:20

Do you imagine that everything must go perfectly for fellowship to be sweet and real? Maybe those times when the "seams" show are really the best . . . for then our pretenses are shattered, and we see each other's lives as the imperfect works-in-progress that they are. Even in chaos God comes in . . . and he makes himself at home.

Living with My Hands Full

$\mathcal{I}$ had to grin when I saw him . . . mostly because I could relate. The fellow coming toward me on the sidewalk just had *way* too much going on at once. He led three bigger-than-average dogs on leashes (or, I should say they led him)—and a boy of about five or six wobbled in front of him on a bike with training wheels. The man was clearly stretched but maintaining equilibrium. Then, at the moment our eyes connected, the dogs went in three different directions, his son's bike hit a slope in the sidewalk, and he grabbed with his free hand for the bike's handlebars just as they began to slide away from him.

If I could have captured him with a camera, I would have put his picture on my refrigerator, with this self-styled caption: *Pay attention. Here's what happens when you try to do too much at once.*

In a world where multitaskers congratulate themselves, busy people are sought after to do still more, and precious few stray moments are left "unbooked," my torn and tethered friend seemed right at home. And most of the time, so do I.

I juggle all kinds of stuff from dawn to dusk. "Still" and "empty-handed" aren't adjectives anyone would be likely to use on my behalf. I frequently overestimate my efficiency and underestimate the length of time it takes to do the simplest things. I cram my days full and carry as much as (or more than) I comfortably can, whether I'm going from room to room or appointment to appointment.

In other words—my dogs are too often going one way and my bike another.

This sidewalk encounter left me with two questions: First, what am I doing that I shouldn't be? And second, what would happen if I stopped?

What would happen if I deliberately made room in any given day or week for . . . nothing? If I emptied my hands of possessions and hobbies and busy work, would my stillness invite anything in? Or make room for anyone? Could there be a blessing God is waiting to give until I empty my hands of my usual "haul"? And finally—wouldn't today be as good a day as any to find out?

What would life be like if I cleared a place for an altar—and found that the only sacrifice my God desired was me? I won't know, will I, until I'm ready to stop living with my hands full?

> Now as they were traveling along, He entered a village; and a woman named Martha welcomed Him into her home. She had a sister called Mary, who was seated at the Lord's feet listening to His word. But Martha was distracted with all her preparations . . . and said, "Lord, do You not care that my sister has left me to do all the serving alone?" . . . But the Lord answered and said to her, "Martha, Martha, you are worried and bothered about so many things; but only one thing is necessary, for Mary has chosen the good part, which shall not be taken away from her."
>
> Luke 10:38–42

We live in a culture that thrives on overcommitment. To be busy is seen as a badge of honor. But maybe there is wisdom in paring down, in cutting back and waiting to see what God would have us do with the space we empty . . . for him.

The Bread and the Wine
Came to Me

*D*uring Holy Week, I attended a sunset Good Friday service at a large, outdoor pavilion. As the biblical account of Jesus's passion was read, three wooden crosses were erected on the hill above the amphitheater, and I watched quietly. There were hundreds already seated with me, waiting for the evening of worship to begin—and hundreds more beyond us on the hill.

Communion was offered, but I couldn't see from my seat who was serving the bread and the cup or how. There didn't seem to be a line, just lots of folks packed shoulder to shoulder about a hundred yards away. I thought of getting up—I wanted to participate—but picking up my stuff and moving seemed too cumbersome, and I was alone, with no one to save my spot for me until I returned. By the time I thought better of it, the crowd on the hill began to disperse, and I imagined the ad hoc offering of bread and wine was done.

While the sun set and the stage was readied, two women walked by—one carrying a large, torn round of bread in a basket, and the second a chunky, clay-fired cup. The person seated behind me stopped them and asked them to serve the elements to her and to her husband, and they did—right there on the aisle, stage right. I wanted to ask too, but I felt suddenly shy—like it might have been too much of an imposition to stop them again.

"The body of Christ," the bread lady whispered to them, then "the blood of the new covenant, shed for you," murmured the woman with the cup, and they turned to walk away. But as she passed my shoulder, the woman with the loaf stopped wordlessly and extended it to me. I tore a piece off, and I dipped my bread in the offered cup. "The body of Christ," they said to me. "The blood of the new covenant."

I placed the morsel in my mouth—sweet and sour at once—and chewed it slowly. I swallowed, but not easily, and my eyes stung with tears. I had wanted that moment, but perhaps not wanted it enough to climb the hill and fumble for it. I had longed for it, but I didn't seek it out. Instead, the bread and the wine came to me.

My small, silent feast was soon swallowed up by the words and music that followed—and they were triumphant and glorious. But Good Friday for me was this: the realization that, when I wanted them most, needed them most, and expended no effort at all to gain them, the bread and the wine came to me. And so did Jesus.

> But God, being rich in mercy, because of His great love with which He loved us, even when we were dead in our transgressions, made us alive together with Christ . . . For by grace you have been saved through faith; and that not of yourselves, it is the gift of God.
>
> Ephesians 2:4–5, 8

How humbling it is to realize that I didn't even come to Jesus on my own! He quickened my heart to love him—to reach for him. I was dead, and could do no reaching of my own. He came to me because I could not come to him.

Don't Supersize Me!

*I*t was an event that had been a long time in the planning, and those responsible had planned well. Nearly a year before the fact, I agreed to travel to another city to speak at a conference for single adults—and when the week arrived, I felt prayed-up and eager to go. There were four other speakers on the agenda—and I was most decidedly *not* the star attraction. Others whose names were readily recognized were slated to speak before me, and I was glad for this.

Well, I was glad until I saw the first speaker projected on a gi-normous (that's giant *and* enormous) big screen behind the podium while she spoke, and every subsequent speaker likewise. Not that they didn't look great "high and lifted up." They did. What unnerved me was that in a few short hours, *I'd* be that big and looming down on my real, smaller self—and I had no desire to be supersized in front of a lot of people I didn't know. (Who would, really?)

The screen and its intimidating size reminded me that sometimes we project the people on the podium to be larger-than-life . . . and they're not. *I'm* not. We're all flawed and a little fragile, sometimes afraid and utterly human. We just happen to have a very big God. My job is chiefly this: to point to *him* and say, "Look at him. Isn't he *something?*"

The night before my turn on the jumbo-tron, I very carefully arched my eyebrows. (Okay, like I said, I'm human.) And I thought a bit more than I might have about how well my clothes fit. But here's the great thing: once I stood up, I was never tempted to peek at "big me." (I was, however, tempted to say in a booming voice, á la the exposed huckster in *The Wizard of Oz*, "Pay no attention to the twenty-foot talking torso before you.")

"Big me" was at my back, and I could only hope she wasn't too distracting. Because "mini-me" had something to say on behalf of great-big God, and I didn't want anyone to mistake the show for the message. We do that sometimes. We supersize the messenger and shrink the message. We applaud the speaker and forget the Word. We think too much of ourselves and far, far too little of him.

As painful as it was to be supersized, I'm glad for the uncomfortable experience. It reminded me that there is a decided downside to being made "big." And that there is only One who is meant to be high and lifted up. It's not me. It will *never* be me. It was ever him and always will be. I'm so grateful that it's so.

> But may it never be that I would boast, except in the cross of our Lord Jesus Christ, through which the world has been crucified to me, and I to the world.
>
> Galatians 6:14

Popularity can be deceiving, and praise downright addictive. In a culture that worships its heroes with alarming zeal (and scant discretion), even faith-talkers are not immune to being "supersized." Pastors speak on screens that obscure the smaller person behind the pulpit. Artists lead worship on stadium-sized stages. At times, medium and messenger obscure the true object of our focus. But perhaps the even more dangerous threat is that we ourselves will become comfortable with being made "large."

Called to Small

$\mathcal{I}$ had attended a stadium-sized gathering of believers that was compelling and worshipful, and well orchestrated and . . . huge. Teaching, music, prayers, and worship were offered up to our King in a big way. He was rightly honored. I was duly blessed.

As I drove away with a dear friend, we processed together what we had experienced. We're both writers and teachers. Our venues are considerably different. But God has uniquely gifted us both for the things he has called us to do. Only, after the evening we experienced, I began to wonder if maybe my gifts were lacking, somehow. If my offerings weren't more meager and insignificant than even I had realized. I don't teach thousands; I teach a handful at a time. And my musical gifts could barely fill a thimble, although music moves my heart deeply.

Could God possibly, after receiving glory and praise and honor in such an over-the-top way, be pleased with what little I have to give him? I think so. And the reason I think so is this: some are called to big . . . and they come through in a big way. Praise him that they do! I think (and I have for some time now) that I may be called to small. And I want him to get glory in that too.

I feel most at home in living rooms and coffee shops and hallways and rooms too small to bother with a microphone. I sometimes find myself in larger spaces. And that's okay. But I'm still the girl who gets overwhelmed at loud parties and searches for a quiet corner. And after I've heard great teaching and been a participant in anointed worship, what I need most is to steal away alone and reflect on the glory I've just seen and prayed about, and sung and said "amen" to.

After being a part of such a great gathering, I felt no small amount of shame that I have not honored God in bigger ways. But a few days later, I came afresh to this passage in Matthew's Gospel: "He presented another parable to them, saying, 'The kingdom of heaven is like a mustard seed, which a man took and sowed in his field; and this is smaller than all other seeds, but when it is full grown, it is larger than the garden plants and becomes a tree, so that the birds of the air come and nest in its branches.'" (Matt. 13:31–32).

What I hope God will do with the smallish deposits of his glorious kingdom that reside in me is to grow them just big enough. Big enough for him to get the glory he deserves, but small enough for me to avoid the glory I *don't* deserve. Big enough to be shelter for anyone who needs the support of its branches or to rest in its shade. Big enough to stay small, lest I should be confused about whose kingdom this *really* is.

So I praise him for my gifts and how they're offered. He is more than big enough to get from them the honor he so rightly deserves.

> Two things I asked of You, do not refuse me before I die: keep deception and lies far from me, give me neither poverty nor riches; feed me with the food that is my portion, that I not be full and deny You and say, "Who is the LORD?" Or that I not be in want and steal and profane the name of my God.
>
> Proverbs 30:7–9

I have been given enough. You have been given enough. You needn't be a second-class version of anyone else, nor should I. There is no shame in how we were made. Our challenge is to use what is ours to the glory of the Giver—not to measure ourselves against someone else's assignment.

The Loveliest Ruins

The most beautiful things I've seen lately might, at first glance, seem spoiled.

Maybe that's because our buffed, airbrushed, and artfully arranged culture leaves scant room for anything it deems less than perfect.

Just days ago I noticed the peonies I paid too much a stem for out-of-season are dying in the most exquisite way: leaving their silky, fragrant, and feathery petals in pools of red on the dining room table. Each morning a few more fall, until now there are great handfuls of them . . . so lovely I can't bear to pick them up and toss them away.

Last week I visited a seventeen-year-old in the hospital; she is giving cancer a run for its money and seems to be winning. Except her hair is gone, save the softest, frizziest stuff that doesn't keep her skull from showing through . . . and radiation has left mean scars on her neck where the skin was once soft and smooth.

Here's what I noticed, as I watched her speak in a voice that never wavered: her eyes were luminous, brilliant blue—and her smile was quick, and real. I couldn't get over how pretty she looked, curled up in flannel pajama pants and a baseball T-shirt, chattering away as if we were somewhere else—and neither of us was sick.

Then I stumbled upon these words from a Martin Luther sermon given at the parish church of Wittenberg on Christmas Day 1534: " 'Unto you,' states the angel, 'is born a Savior, which is Christ the Lord.' These words melt heaven and earth together, make death into sugar, and turn all ills, of which there are plenty, into delectable wine."

Christ is the One who makes the difference. He is the Savior who transforms the broken and dying into the beautiful and blessed. Who makes loss sweet and presses pain and sadness into the very best of wines. We want to turn away from death and ruin and slow decay, but when we do we miss their glory. It is when we see them as they are that all their beauty blazes through. Not until, and never before. And because our Savior has disarmed death and left its wrappings behind like drifts of flower petals, hope lodges deep in every lovely ruin.

> But we have this treasure in earthen vessels, so that the surpassing greatness of the power will be of God and not from ourselves; we are afflicted in every way, but not crushed; perplexed, but not despairing; persecuted, but not forsaken; struck down, but not destroyed; always carrying about in the body the dying of Jesus, so that the life of Jesus also may be manifested in our body. . . . Therefore we do not lose heart, but though our outer man is decaying, yet our inner man is being renewed day by day . . . for the things which are seen are temporal, but the things which are not seen are eternal.
>
> 2 Corinthians 4:7–10, 16, 18

Delectable wine. Our "ills" — in light of Christ's incarnation — are delectable wine. Because he came to identify with us in our ruin, we can identify with him in his resurrected glory. That's not denial. It's redemption.

Working around the Repairs

*F*or several days in a row, my home has looked (and sounded) more like a war zone than a sanctuary. As I write these words, my living and dining room furniture has been "dispatched" to bedrooms, hallway, and kitchen, and no matter how often I sweep, my adorable dust mop of a dog collects tiny flecks of sawdust in his coat that he distributes wherever he goes.

The repairs to the hardwood floors in my old duplex have taken twice as long as promised (isn't that always the way it goes?), and my patience has stretched only half as far as I'd hoped.

I don't mind admitting that I like order. I like things in their place and looking lovely. I like working to the sound of music or the muted street noise outside my window—not (I've discovered) to the screeching of an electric saw and the dull pounding of a rubber mallet. And while I'm certain the result of all this noise and mess and confusion will be pleasing, the process is really *not*. Not at all.

Isn't life a lot like that? We want things to be a certain way, to have a certain look and feel—and so very often they aren't . . . and don't. We'd prefer less confusion and more order. Less chaos and more calm. Less pounding and banging . . . and more harps and strings. We'd like that—but for the most part, we're all under construction or renovation. And we simply work around the repairs.

God knows the end result he's after . . . and he has his tools assembled and ready. Sometimes there's tearing-out work to be done. Old things must be removed to make room for new. Those tearing-out tools can be downright scary when used with force.

And what gets torn out isn't always immediately replaced, so we learn to live with empty patches until the master-craftsman fills them in.

Then after the major renovation/repair—the ripping up and replacing—is complete, the finishing begins. "Finishing." Doesn't that sound nice and soft? It isn't. It involves sanding and staining and thousands of even, repetitive strokes until rough edges are smooth and uneven grains are matched.

If I were God (and this is the place where we should all stop and breathe thanks that I am *not!*), I might have been tempted just to start over from scratch. After all, wouldn't it be easier to create exactly what you want to begin with, than to chip away at what you *don't* want a little at a time? But the very fact that he could do it that way—and doesn't—makes me certain he values the process. And me.

And that he's quite content to allow me to work as he repairs.

> And coming to Him as to a living stone which has been rejected by men, but is choice and precious in the sight of God, you also, as living stones, are being built up as a spiritual house for a holy priesthood, to offer up spiritual sacrifices acceptable to God through Jesus Christ.
>
> 1 Peter 2:4–5

I've always wondered why God didn't just make us perfect people to begin with. All along he knew that we'd need not just saving—but sanctifying. And he's perfectly fine with the lengthy process required—we're the ones that struggle with it. Are you frustrated with the time and trouble of being made into the image of Christ? Can you think of anything more worthwhile you might be doing instead?

Sounding Out the Words

I'd almost forgotten phonics. It had been a long time since I'd sounded out words in pieces in order to read them. But when a dear friend's son read aloud to me from a beginner's storybook, it all came rushing back. I don't recall the name of the book, or truthfully, even the contents of the story. Those things weren't the point. The point was that the first-grader leaning over the book in my lap was learning—stringing the sounds into words and the words into sentences, so that one day stories would make sense.

It was a beautiful struggle and a fine beginning.

I'd almost forgotten that I learned "catch" by forming a hard "k" sound, then following it with an "eh," and then a "ch." And that a word like "weighs" is a lot harder than "ways" to figure out. But I remembered the satisfaction of a hard sentence completed and a new page turned. And of how good it felt to hear my teacher say, "That's right—good job!"

I'm light-years past phonics in the reading department. As I look around the books that surround my study floor to ceiling, it sobers me to think how long reading would take (and how utterly unsatisfying it would be) if I still relied on phonics to complete each one. But I haven't entirely put the tool away.

I revisit grade school often in my faith. When I'm faced with a new and perplexing situation, I remember a particular combination of truths or events from the past, and I sound out the right response. When I'm frightened by challenging circumstances, I pull up from memory words I've come to know by heart that speak directly to my fear. When I don't know where to go or what to do, I search for patterns from the past and turn the dog-eared pages of my primer/storybook to find direction. And it's there.

So now you have the truth. I'm still hooked on phonics. But I'm looking forward—so forward!—to the day when what I sometimes still must sound out haltingly will be spoken fluently. When I can put the book away and find every answer I need in the face of my good Teacher. When his great, wild story—and not just bits and pieces of it—will make perfect sense to me . . . and every struggle, large or small, will be more than worth the effort.

173

One day I will be his star pupil. Until then, I am content to wrestle with my words so that I may learn to love him more.

> For we know in part and we prophesy in part, but when perfection comes, the imperfect disappears. When I was a child, I talked like a child, I thought like a child, I reasoned like a child. When I became a man, I put childish ways behind me. Now we see but a poor reflection as in a mirror; then we shall see face to face. Now I know in part; then I shall know fully, even as I am fully known.
>
> 1 Corinthians 13:9–12 NIV

Are you struggling to put sentences of faith together, still? Keep reading. Keep sounding out the words. The Teacher is listening, and he delights to hear your progress, and mine.

When Chester Smiled

My dog Chester smiled. He really did. He had two smiles, actually. One was an open-mouthed, tongue-hanging-out grin that he reserved for company. He went temporarily berserk when the doorbell rang, ran madly through the living room until all guests had been "herded" in and seated, then parked himself in front of the one he deemed most amenable to him and turned on the goofy charm.

I don't know what he might have been thinking (or *if* he was thinking), but his "company" smile seemed to say, "Wow! That was exhilarating! Now it's time for you to tell me how much you appreciated my energetic performance and how desperately cute you think I am!" (Most guests obliged.)

Chester's company smile made me laugh—but it was not the one I liked best.

The Chester-smile that was my favorite was the one he smiled only for me. He had to be really relaxed for it, and warm. Mornings or late evenings were best. Stretched out on the sofa or the foot of the bed, he'd sigh and roll belly-up, paws next to his chest. That was the signal for the full-body "scruff." I'd ruffle his silky hair, starting at his ears, then move under his chin, over his ribs, and down his back. By the time I got to his tail, his eyes were closed, his mouth was shut, and the corners of it were slightly—oh, so slightly—inching upward into a smile. He smiled for as long as I would scratch.

That was the deal.

Chester's two smiles got me thinking: I wonder if I have a smile that pleases God the most? Is it my "performance" smile? The "I'm so happy to be a Christian and my life is just about perfect, thank you very much" smile? Is it my "doing good deeds" smile? The one that works its way onto my face when I'm doing something I'm pretty sure God will be pleased with?

Or is it the one that no one else sees—the smile that barely shows on the outside but wells up from deep within, when the One who knows me best touches a hidden place in my heart and leaves his hand there just long enough to warm me all the way through? That quiet smile that's triggered by a memory, or music, or a smell, or a snippet of words that sound just right?

I can't say for sure—but I think it's the latter that he most enjoys. Because it's the one he—and he alone—is responsible for.

You will make known to me the path of life; in Your presence is fullness of joy; in Your right hand there are pleasures forever.

Psalm 16:11

God wants me to take pleasure in him. He wants me to be deeply and fully satisfied with him. Those who would say he's interested only in their sacrifice or their services haven't yet experienced his true heart.

Wrestling the Tree

Every year, envisioning a tall, sturdy, fresh-smelling fir tucked in the corner of my living room, I do significant recon on where the most reasonably priced specimen can be found and make the annual expedition to the tree lot. Then, after looking at and handling no less than a dozen viable candidates, I select one tree to take home with me. Usually I've chosen a lot whose workers will hoist my purchase to the top of the car and tie it down, but after that, it's do-it-yourself all the way home and beyond.

Each time I repeat this drill, I acknowledge that setting up a Christmas tree is no one-man (or in this case, one-woman) job.

I could ask for help, of course. But there's something about this me-and-the-tree duel that sucks me in every time. I see no reason why I shouldn't be able to outwit, outmaneuver, and outmuscle the process *and* the tree, whose size I almost always regret as soon as I've gotten it home. (Charlie Brown I am not when it comes to selecting trees.)

Along the way, I've learned a few tree-wrestling lessons that have proved helpful. Rolling the tree off your car from the side is a great deal safer than grasping the base of the trunk and pulling it toward you (don't ask). Putting the stand *on* the tree while it's horizontal is infinitely easier than placing the tree *in* the stand while attempting to keep it vertical. And, a kind of "walking hug" is the safest (albeit most awkward) way of getting said tree through whatever doorway you've selected as your initial point of entry.

This year I wrestled the tree again, and the experience got me thinking. I struggle against my Christmas tree once a year. But it's really me-and-the-tree all year long. The tree I wrestle daily is my own cross, which I've been commanded to take up and carry with me, looking for opportunities to climb upon it often, and allow myself to die.

The cross is also a tree I both love and struggle against. I love its beauty, and I struggle against its stark invitation. I love its power, and struggle against its authority. I love its mercy, and yet struggle against its grace. It's not easy, this wrestling with the tree. Dietrich Bonhoeffer said, "When Christ calls a man, he bids him come and die." And why shouldn't he? He's already done it himself.

I resist help with my Christmas tree. But I'd be a fool to resist help with my cross. Even Jesus accepted help with his. And when I've overestimated my own ability or strength or resolve, or when the whole process has left me exhausted and scraped up and scared, the One who's gone before me sees, and says, "Lovely, lovely tree. But it's big, and you're small. Can I help you with that?"

> He forgave us all our sins, having canceled the written code, with its regulations, that was against us and that stood opposed to us; he took it away, nailing it to the cross. And having disarmed the powers and authorities, he made a public spectacle of them, triumphing over them by the cross.
>
> Colossians 2:13–15, NIV

*Do you struggle against the cross? It's an awful offense,
isn't it? We decorate all manner of things with it—but
truthfully, it's a symbol of terrible struggle and a cruel
death. And it's one we're called to identify wholly with until
the day we die. But not alone. Never, ever alone.*

Turbulence

*I*t was one of those rides you don't soon forget. The
plane was shaking and shimmying and bumping in new
and alarming ways—and I hadn't seen a flight attendant
since takeoff. The "fasten seat belt" sign was still glowing overhead, and the passengers who'd resolutely affixed
ear pods upon boarding to avoid background noise or un-
wanted conversation were removing them, in hopes of
hearing a reassuring announcement from the cockpit.

Those of us who were trying to look nonchalant (as in,
"I'm a seasoned traveler; this is nothing unusual") were fail-
ing . . . miserably. I could see nothing outside the window
to either confirm or deny that we were in distress. Truth
told, I wouldn't even know what to look for.

The announcement that finally came was not the one I
hoped for. "Ladies and gentlemen, the captain has advised
that we are experiencing some temporary turbulence. He
will remove the fasten-seat-belt sign when it is safe to do
so." Duh. No enlightenment there. What I was anticipat-
ing was an explanation as to what sort of conditions were
producing a ride that made a 737 feel like a two-man fishing
boat. And especially how long they might last.

The next word from the flight crew was no better: "Ladies
and gentlemen, we will be suspending beverage service
temporarily. When service resumes, no hot beverages will

be served. Please remain in your seats until the captain has turned off the fasten-seat-belt sign, and do not open the overhead bins."

I didn't care about beverage service. And I had nothing stowed in the overhead bin to begin with. I wanted to know one thing, and one thing only: What does the captain of this plane think of our situation? What does he have to say about the weather, his ability to navigate safely through it, and its impact on our intended arrival time? What is *his* take on the storm?

I have no special power over large airplanes, or the winds that buffet them. I have no skill in flight control or the ability to predict the impact of a storm. But I know my Captain. And when my journey is perilous and my safety is in doubt, I want only to hear from him. What does he think of my situation? What does he see that I cannot? How will he lift me over the storm, steer me around it, or bear me safely through it?

It's his voice I'm waiting for—and his steady, faithful, confident words I most need to hear. Because he—and only he—is sovereign over turbulence.

> But as they were sailing along He fell asleep; and a fierce gale of wind descended on the lake, and they began to be swamped and to be in danger. They came to Jesus and woke Him up, saying, "Master, Master, we are perishing!" And He got up and rebuked the wind and the surging waves, and they stopped, and it became calm.
>
> Luke 8:23–24

I love what the disciples said to one another after their rescue from turbulent seas: "Who then is this, that He commands even the winds and the water, and they obey Him?" (v. 25). They knew him, of course. He was no stranger to them. He was Jesus, of Galilee. But they didn't

179

yet know the extent of his power, or that the One who spoke the worlds into being slept safely in their tiny boat!

Sealed with a Kiss

*L*ately, I've been noticing kisses. No, I'm not devouring romance novels, Tivo-ing the soaps, or indulging in one too many romantic comedies. (Although I *will* watch *You've Got Mail* for the umpteenth time on television just because it's on.)

Most mornings, I see moms kiss their kids good-bye after walking them to the gate of the elementary school at the end of my block. Sometimes the kids forget their kiss and run back for it. (This makes the crossing guard's job a little more complex.)

If I didn't have an adorable dog of my own, I'd be amazed at how many people kiss their pets. A kiss a day is, of course, a requirement for Chester the Japanese Chin, who came with his own ready-made "kissing spot"—a small white wisp of fur right on the top of his softball-sized head.

Then there are, of course, the obligatory wedding ceremony kisses—front and center—that declare to all that the deal is done. Sometimes they're funny, sometimes sweet, and sometimes over-the-top exuberant.

But the kiss that got me thinking—and noticing all these other kisses—was the kiss that "fingered" the Son of God and sounded the starting gun for his terrible, beautiful surrender: "Immediately while He was still speaking, Judas, one of the twelve, came up accompanied by a crowd with swords and clubs, who were from the chief priests and the scribes and the elders. Now he who was betraying Him had given them a signal, saying, 'Whomever I kiss, He is the one; seize Him and lead Him away under guard.' After coming, Judas immediately went to Him, saying, 'Rabbi!' and kissed Him. They laid hands on Him, and seized Him" (Mark 14:43–46).

All my life I've read of the five wounds of Christ . . . but really, weren't there six? And was the kiss he received from one of his own beloved men any less piercing than the wounds Jesus bore in his hands and feet and side?

How could he? I think when I consider Judas's kiss. How could he say "Rabbi!" and smile and touch God's very cheek with a sign of honor when in his heart he knew that he was selling him out? How could he? And it was Judas himself who chose the sign of the kiss! I would have pointed, with my hand close to my ribs, that this one was the One. Or nodded my head curtly in his direction and then looked away.

How do I know? Because that's precisely how I sin. Slyly. Covertly. With small, close-to-the-vest motions, not broad, sweeping ones. With averted eyes. Not with open kisses. But perhaps it's time to rethink that strategy. Maybe I should *consider* a kiss each time I consider sin. Maybe if I saw myself—with my fickle, betraying heart—sidle up to the Son of God and kiss him each time I contemplated choosing my own way over his, I'd sin less.

Maybe if I thought of the great love that set me free I'd fall on my own face in repentance before I'd kiss his in deliberate denial.

Lately, I've been noticing kisses.

But Jesus said to him, "Judas, are you betraying the Son of Man with a kiss?"

Luke 22:48

Because I belong to Jesus, each time I sin I repeat Judas's betraying kiss. Sure, I feign affection, allegiance even—but

I can throw him over when it suits me. He would ask the
same question of me that he asked of his early disciple: "Are
you betraying me with a kiss?" Say it isn't so!

A Freakish Storm

*I*f you don't like the weather," they say about Texas,
"wait a few hours, and it will change." My corner of the map
experienced that southern unpredictability recently when
a jumbled mix of violent weather that local weathercasters
called "a freakish storm" struck our city. It lasted only a
few hours, but before it relented, the storm had wreaked
havoc with torrential rain, tornadoes, and massive traffic
jams caused by flash floods.

The morning after the tempest brought the bluest sky
we'd had in months, and the kind of crisp, cool air that had
as yet been missing from November. Monday I couldn't
have seen ten feet in front of my face. Tuesday dawned
with clear-as-a-bell beauty as far as the eye could see.
But it wasn't the typical, still beauty of the calm after the
storm.

The wind blew hard enough to suspend leaves and lit-
ter midair, creating swirling patterns above my head. The
branches of the trees on my block waved and sighed, and
a great many of the smaller ones let go their hold and
clattered to the sidewalk like pickup sticks as I watched.
Moments after I came inside, a branch from the huge oak
in the front yard cracked and fell with a massive thud in
the yard, not five feet from where I'd stood. If it had hit me,
it would have knocked me senseless. But nothing about
the day looked threatening. Nothing at all.

The storm that paralyzed my city for a few hours on Monday was dangerous, and it damaged what you would expect such a storm to damage. But on my street, Tuesday left more broken things—and Tuesday was absolutely lovely.

When life serves up freakish storms we hunker down in the safest places we know and prepare for the worst. We get our game faces on, and resolve to ride out the chaos of a sudden illness or an ugly divorce, the death of a loved one or financial ruin. And mostly, we do. We manage. We get by. We survive. The days that trail disaster often dawn bright and clear, and when we see the clouds lift, we breathe a huge sigh of relief. "Maybe that's the worst of it," we tell ourselves. "Maybe now I'll be all right."

We fool ourselves.

Branches fall on bright, blue days. Things get broken, even in the midst of beauty. "We live on holy ground," writes Eugene Peterson. "We inhabit sacred space. This holy ground is subject to incredible violations. This sacred space suffers constant sacrilege. But no matter. The holiness is there, the sacredness is there."[1]

There are freakish storms that we can track—and freakish winds we can't predict. We are blessed and battered by both, and we control neither. Because the wind has always been Someone else's domain.

> Have you ever in your life commanded the
>   morning,
>   And caused the dawn to know its place,
> That it might take hold of the ends of the earth,
>   And the wicked be shaken out of it? . . .
> Have you entered the storehouses of the snow,
>   Or have you seen the storehouses of hail? . . .
> Who has cleft a channel for the flood,
>   Or a way for the thunderbolt? . . .
> Can you lift up your voice to the clouds,
>   So that an abundance of water will cover
>   you?

Can you send forth lightnings that they may
   go
And say to you, "Here we are"?

Job 38:12–13, 22, 25, 34–35

This life is so unpredictable. Our creature comforts can insulate us from most inclement days, but there are dangers about whether we sense them or not. Still, as Peterson says, "We inhabit sacred space." The power of nature is a reminder of the power of our Maker. This is his world—holy and wild. We cannot presume to temper or control it. That is for God alone.

Watch This! Watch This!

I was a performing child, and I remember performing well—not only because I wanted the satisfaction of doing a thing rightly but because I wanted the praise that typically comes with achievement. I made straight A's, kept my elbows off the table, crossed my legs at the ankle, and said "Yes ma'am" and "Yes sir" to my elders. I did my homework on time, my chores when told, and (minus a couple of instances that are legend in the family book of deeds) kept my curfew without grumbling.

Because I performed well, I think my parents were mostly pleased. They praised my efforts and my accomplishments, and I liked that very much. But I also believe—although I never tested them too rigorously on this—that they would have loved me just as much had I *not* performed so well. I believe this because I love the children in my life, even when they don't shine.

Whether they are grumpy or belligerent, sad or silly, disobedient or disinterested, I applaud their achievements like my parents applauded mine—but I adore them in any circumstance because of the bond between us, nothing more. I would go anywhere, pay any price, endure any heartbreak if their good was at stake—and I know God feels just that way about me.

I don't have to keep topping my own personal best to get (or keep) his approval. I don't have to call out "Watch this! Watch this!" to command his attention. I don't need to worry that failure will cause him to fall out of love with me, because I am his child.

"God doesn't need to be dazzled," Emilie Griffin writes. "God already delights in you."[2]

When my oldest niece graduated from high school with high honors, I sat through seven hundred other graduates' names before I heard hers called (she's a "W") and started crying in the middle of the "R's." Somehow, I don't think it discredits any of her many achievements to say I would have felt the same way if she'd have been last in her class and arrived at the ceremony on a Harley. Am I proud of what she's done? You bet. Do I love who she is? Even more than I can say.

The day after Katharine's graduation, I took another eighteen-year-old I'd known for a few very short months to dinner. His list of accomplishments is not so very long. His past is messier than most. I tried not to wince when he lifted his shoulder-length hair to show me his half-shaved skull underneath. "I did it myself," he said grinning. But midway through our meal when he looked me in the eye and said, "Thanks for this; I love hanging out with you," I was swallowing tears again.

There's a lot I don't know, because I'm not a mom. But I know this: where love is concerned, it's belonging that counts—not performing.

[Love] bears all things, believes all things, hopes all things, endures all things. Love never fails.

1 Corinthians 13:7–8a

Do you ever feel the need to "dazzle" God? What could you do that could make him love you more? He has already given everything to make you his.

Just Dessert

Bud and Cathaleen were married more than fifty years, raising three children and enjoying two treasured grandchildren. Bud remembered every one of those years to his final day, but Parkinson's disease and a debilitating stroke erased Cathaleen's memory long before it claimed her body.

After these challenges had altered her personality and severely limited her ability to do simple tasks, her husband cared for her every day. He bathed and dressed her, combed her hair, and fed her in the place she wanted most to be—the home he built with his own hands. Their children did what they could for their parents, but Bud was most comfortable when he was her chief caregiver, and so was Cathaleen.

Bud talked to Cathaleen. Held her hand. Drove her to the beauty parlor and cooked her favorite foods. Her looks and nature had changed greatly, but his devotion never wavered. He never kept score. He lived with her moment by moment, and at any given moment, in his eyes, the slate was fresh and clean.

On one of their last holidays together, they shared dinner in the home of their two daughters, who had made the table as pretty as they could—and as uncluttered and spill proof as their mother needed. Their father helped her with her food, as he had done for some time. After dinner, the daughters cleared the table for coffee and dessert. When they served pie, Cathaleen tumbled her slice off her plate and onto the table, then began to eat it off the tablecloth.

Brushing aside his daughters' hurried attempts to set things right, Bud simply smiled and slid his own dessert onto the table, patted his wife's hand, and topped both of their pie slices with big dollops of whipped cream. They finished their desserts together.

G. K. Chesterton wrote, "The thing which keeps life romantic and full of fiery possibilities is the existence of these great plain limitations, which force all of us to meet the things we do not like or do not expect."

This elderly husband never expected to have an invalid wife for nearly fifteen years. He never foresaw losing the ability to converse and reminisce with her. No doubt some days he did not like it. But he never quit. And he never complained.

We cannot know if we have the "stuff" to truly love until we meet the moment that calls for love. But we have the example we need if we ever hope to triumph: "We love, because He first loved us" (1 John 4:19).

> Love never gives up. Love cares more for others than for self. Love doesn't want what it doesn't have . . . puts up with anything, trusts God always, always looks for the best, never looks back, but keeps going to the end.
>
> 1 Corinthians 13:4–7 Message

Love adjusts. Accepts. Flexes. Persists. If it didn't, it would surely shatter from the pressures of ordinary life. When I see this kind of love in action, I want to imitate it. Today will surely offer me a moment—or many—to practice what I've learned.

Passing by the Dragon

When I was little, I used to run past the stuff I was afraid of. Dark rooms, big bugs, mean dogs—anything that frightened me I consistently passed by with as much speed as I could muster. The faster I moved, I reasoned, the less chance there was of the scary thing "getting" me.

We're all a little (or a lot) afraid of something. Even as grown-ups. Maybe it's crime, or natural disaster. Or maybe cancer terrifies us—or heart disease. Perhaps abandonment is a big dark room to some, or change, or hunger or solitude. We're not just frightened for ourselves, either. We fear for our loved ones too—and for the hidden dangers we can't see or name but know are out there just the same.

Flannery O'Connor found a name for this in the writings of St. Cyril of Jerusalem, who called it "passing by the dragon." In St. Cyril's words, "The dragon sits by the side of the road, watching those who pass. Beware lest he devour you. We go to the Father of Souls, but it is necessary to pass by the dragon."

O'Connor added, "No matter what form the dragon may take, it is of this mysterious passage past him, or into his jaws, that stories of any depth will always be concerned to tell . . . and it requires considerable courage at any time . . . not to turn away from the storyteller."[3]

Fear is natural, whether you're young or old. But living in fear of fear is not. Arranging my days to avoid anything that might make my heart flutter out of time, or my breath become quick and shallow, is not really living at all. Real living takes real courage, and real courage comes from knowing that God is present in every crisis—that "we go to the Father of Souls." Shepherd/warrior/king David said it this way: "Even when the way goes through Death Valley, I'm not afraid when you walk at my side. Your trusty shepherd's crook makes me feel secure. You serve me a six-course dinner right in front of my enemies. You revive my drooping head; my cup brims with blessing" (Ps. 23:4–5 Message).

Those adrenalin-infused moments when we are passing by the dragon are the very times that our Father of Souls is nearest, ready with whatever it is we need most. And those are the times that our life takes on a depth and wildness that seasons us, and makes our stories rich and full.

Is the dragon near? Can you feel his hot breath and hear his heavy, thundering steps? Take heart. You are traveling *through* the valley. You are passing *by* the dragon. You are going *to* the Father of Souls, who is, even in this moment, nearer than you know.

> The steps of a man are established by the LORD, and He delights in his way. When he falls, he will not be hurled headlong, because the LORD is the One who holds his hand.
>
> Psalm 37:23–24

Does your dragon have a name? Is he near? Remember the Shepherd who walks by your side and comforts you with his crook. St. Patrick said it this way: "Christ with me, Christ before me, Christ behind me, Christ within me, Christ beneath me, Christ above me, Christ at my right, Christ at my left." Breathe deeply. The dragon may be closing in, but you are surrounded by your King—and he is very brave.

Face Time

In spite of all the communication gizmos at our disposal, there's just no substitute for face time. Instant messaging, voice mail, email, and blogging may fool us into thinking we're connected—solidly connected—with another human being, but these tools are illusory. Used unsparingly for anything but the most basic exchanges of information, they can make us a mile wide and an inch deep.

I spoke on the phone recently to a friend in another state, and realizing I didn't have his new email address, asked for it. "Sure," he said, "but I prefer to talk. If this were an email, I couldn't hear you laugh, or pick up the tone in your voice, or know how many seconds went by before I asked, and you answered."

Fair enough. Flattering even.

Technology can cause me to think I've "connected" with dozens of people during the course of a day, when I haven't sat for more than a moment before a single living being. These tools may make me efficient, but they don't help me to know deeply or be deeply known.

That takes the commodity we hold most precious of all: time.

My Outlook address book is overflowing. (I've emailed lots of folks, and lots of folks have emailed me.) But my handwritten address book isn't. You make *that* one when you've logged time—face time. When I write your name in pen . . . you're in. When three phone numbers, your snail mail, and your birthday (maybe even your parents' names or addresses) are scratched in, you're known. And I plan to invest the time it takes to keep on knowing you.

Is it any wonder, given our manic reliance on disembodied communication, that we imagine we can somehow know God apart from spending time in his presence? Reading a theology book is a useful pursuit, but that knowledge will take me only so far if it's not matched by time spent in adoration or praise or confession or pleading before the One I've been reading up on.

I'm becoming more and more convinced that my commitment to God is evidenced by my willingness to "waste" time—long stretches of it—before his face. An old hymn I remember from childhood says, "I ask no other sunshine than the sunshine of His face." That's a holy hunger that's not easily satisfied with distant, fleeting things. That's a yearning for "face time" and a confession that nothing less will do. So today, sit still and expectantly before the face of the One who never drifts, and whose love never wanes. And when you think you've been there long enough, linger just a little while more.

> When You said, "Seek My face," my heart said to You, "Your face, O LORD, I shall seek."
>
> Psalm 27:8

If these words have resonated with you . . . don't just be glad that you and I "connected." Talk to someone about them over coffee. Ask a co-worker what he or she thinks of them. Or call a friend you've drifted from and simply listen . . . for as long as it takes to hear what you've been missing.

Keeping Score

I've been asked a few times what my first job was. Since I've had several that might have counted as "firsts," I generally just choose one. My first job out of college was as a junior copywriter at an advertising agency. My first job *in* college was as a television news reporter at a university-owned station. My first part-time job in high school was as a checker at a neighborhood drugstore—back when you (and not a machine) had to know how to make change!

But the first job I was ever paid for, I got when I was thirteen: keeping score at Little League baseball games, for $5 a game.

The games never went more than six innings and were sometimes called sooner because of time. The equipment was simple: a brown, spiral-bound scorekeeper's book, a sharp pencil, and a lawn chair. (Scorekeepers got a free sno-cone at the concession stand after all their games were done.)

On a good Saturday, you could make $15. The hazards were minimal: a stray foul pop over the backstop to dodge, or the occasional grousing parent who wanted to argue the hit or error you might have just scored on their young boy wonder. My Little League experience led to a four-year gig as scorekeeper for my high school's varsity baseball team, where the games were longer, the stakes were higher, and they hit and threw a *lot* harder.

To this day, it's almost impossible for me to watch a baseball game (Little League, high school, college, or pro) without keeping score. And it bugs me when I miss a pitch or a substitution, or pick up the next inning with the wrong batter.

I think I might be a closet legalist.

I want my record to be the last word on who's who and what's what. I want to fill in the book on every contest. I want to hold in my lap the undisputed truth, and to know with finality who's won. Only, it doesn't always work like that in life, does it? And although Little League scorekeeping made me happy, I've found that real-life scorekeeping is a sure and quick road to misery.

I'm not the one keeping the life-book. But it is being kept. And there are no mistakes in it. None at all. My own errors (and there have been plenty) are recorded, and I will be able to see each one. But they have not been charged against me in the final tally. I don't know the divine shorthand—but I'm picturing a little "g" with a circle around it next to my name. In his book, it will stand for *grace*.

> How blessed is he whose transgression is forgiven, whose sin is covered! How blessed is the man to whom the LORD does not impute iniquity, and in whose spirit there is no deceit!
>
> Psalm 32:1–2

Are you a scorekeeper too? A bit of a legalist who wants everything assigned and accounted for? If you're like me, you're more willing to let your own errors slide, and you're a huge fan of justice . . . for everyone else. Remember that we have a righteous Judge. He never misses a call. He always gets it right. And—praise him!—he has held no marks against me.

Part 5

Ordinary Words

Why?

$\mathcal{S}$he said, "I shall know why, when Time is over/ And I have ceased to wonder why;/Christ will explain each separate anguish/In the fair schoolroom of the sky."[1] Her name was Emily Dickinson, and I began to memorize odd lines of her heady, bewitching verse when I was eight or nine. Many of those lines have remained hibernating in my brain for years, but this one resurfaces with some regularity. Why?

Because I seldom know "why"—do you?

Why cancer? Why hijacked airplanes? Why deadly hurricanes, or widowhood, or infertility or broken hearts or starving children? Not "why?" in a global sense. I can get that. The global answer is that, since Adam, man has wrestled with a sin nature—and because the prince of this fallen world is evil and real. But my "why's" are usually more personal than they are global, and I'll bet yours are too.

"Why did I lose my savings?" or "Why did that car run a red light when my friend's car was entering the intersection?" As selfish as it sounds, I don't ache to know the "why" of world hunger as much as I do the why of my own immediate heartbreak.

When Job's world began to unravel he must have wondered why. His livestock was lost. His servants were killed, his fields devastated. Then his children were caught in a whirlwind, and they all died together under the same fallen roof. In a matter of days, everything Job had was lost.

His wife suggested he should just get it over with: "Curse God and die." His friends demanded to know what secret sin of his had caused such unmitigated disaster. Job finally did curse the day he was born, but he never cursed his God. Instead, he wished for an audience with the Almighty— and he had his list of questions ready. Then a funny thing happened. God showed up for that interview. But instead of Job asking the questions, God did. He took Job on a virtual tour of the created world, asking, "Where were you when I made all of this?" And, "Job—can you do what I can do? Can you even begin to explain my ways?" Job could not.

God didn't offer any explanations. Nor did he divulge the content of his earlier conversation with Satan regarding Job's testing. (Sometimes there is activity in another, hidden realm—one that does not receive much attention at all on CNN.) When the tour was over, I imagine Job had crumpled up his list of interrogating questions and dropped it somewhere as discreetly as he could. He was surely out of questions. He had seen enough of the "Who" that the "why" didn't matter anymore.

> Then the LORD said to Job, "Will the faultfinder contend with the Almighty? Let him who reproves God answer it." Then Job answered the LORD and said, "Behold, I am insignificant; what can I reply to You? I lay my hand on my mouth."
>
> Job 40:1–4

To me, the beauty of Emily's poem is not the idea that Christ would willingly explain "each separate anguish" once I am face-to-face with him. It's that once I am there, I will have ceased completely to care. The "Who" will one day be answer enough for every one of my "why's."

"Two Ticks. No Dog."

Years ago I was teaching a Sunday school class on a text from Acts—specifically on Paul and Felix's spiritual and political cat and mouse game, as recorded in the twenty-fifth and twenty-sixth chapters of that book. Paul was a prisoner of Rome, but his real enemies were the Jews of the Sanhedrin. They wanted to have him killed. Felix was the governor of Caesarea—a former slave turned freedman, cunning, and newly invested with power.

Paul wanted nothing more than to preach the gospel. In Rome. Felix wanted a bribe from Paul to keep him from being charged and sent to Rome for trial. For two years they circled one another, talking frequently, but resolving nothing. When Felix was finally succeeded in his office by Festus, he gave up the game and left Paul to languish in prison as a parting favor to the Jews.

As I was explaining this, a voice piped up from the back row. In a delightful Louisiana accent, a man I didn't recognize smiled and said slowly and distinctly: "Two ticks. No dog." For a second I was confused. Then people in the class began to chuckle. And I did as well. I'm not sure any reliable commentary would have summed up their situation in quite that way, but I can't imagine a more apt (or colorful) description.

Both of these characters, Paul and Felix, wanted something from the other. But neither was of a mind to give. Two ticks. No dog.

Sometimes no one gets what they want. Sometimes both parties in an exchange have their minds set on what they want to receive, and are unprepared or unwilling to give what the other needs. Agendas are set. Lines are drawn. A standoff ensues. Goodwill is strained. When we're needy we want the *other* person to give. It's always something of a shock to discover that one we've expected to meet us in our need simply can't. Because they're needy too. Two ticks. No dog.

The fellow who said those words years ago became my good friend. He introduced himself to me after class that day and invited me to share a meal with him. He was so winsome and gracious that I joined him. We couldn't have been more different, but I learned a great deal from him. When I needed encouragement, he gave it. When he needed reassurance, I offered that. We both needed to be loved, and through the Christ who resided in him and in me, we were able to give what the other needed. In our flesh, we're takers, all of us—hungry and looking for a host. But in Christ, we can be transformed to givers, becoming broken bread and poured out wine for a hungry world, or for one. He showed us just how it should be done.

> Near the cross of Jesus stood his mother, his mother's sister, Mary the wife of Clopas, and Mary Magdalene. When Jesus saw his mother there, and the disciple whom he loved standing nearby, he said to his mother, "Dear woman, here is your son," and to the disciple, "Here is your mother." From that time on, this disciple took her into his home.
>
> John 19:25–27

I've been in my share of standoffs waiting for the other person to give in. They're seldom very effective and almost always uncomfortable. Now when I do this, my friend's words convict me and remind me that I can't afford NOT to give what another man needs—especially if we happen to be adversaries!

"Tale as Old as Time, Song as Old as Rhyme"

One scene from Walt Disney's *Beauty and the Beast* causes a lump to form in my throat every time I see it—and I've seen it plenty of times. Captive Belle is dancing with the Beast in an empty ballroom. She is lovely, but although he has shined himself up to his very best, he is still a monster. As he holds her gingerly and twirls her around the enormous room, she smiles up into his hideous face, her eyes glowing with warmth.

It's one of those perfect moments where love creeps in against all odds, and insists on staying put. Where beauty is utterly and completely in the eye of the beholder, and not about to budge.

Apparently the appeal of that particular cinematic moment transcends age or stage of life. I took my two nieces to see the movie when they were seven and eleven, and on the way home I asked them what part they liked best. Seven-year-old Victoria answered from the backseat without a second's hesitation: "Oh, Aunt Leigh! I loved it when she danced with him—*and he was still the Beast!*"

I very nearly wept again.

The film's scorers underlined this scene with the perfect musical truth: *Beauty and the Beast* really *is* a tale as old as time. And the oldest, truest version of it goes something like this: "You see, at just the right time, when we were still powerless, Christ died for the ungodly. Very rarely will anyone die for a righteous man, though for a good man someone might possibly dare to die. But God demonstrates his own love for us in this: While we were still sinners, Christ died for us" (Rom. 5:6–8 NIV).

Who doesn't long to be loved when they're hopelessly unlovely? Who doesn't hope for a savior in the wings who sees them at their very worst and steadfastly refuses to be repulsed? Belle loved the Beast before there was even an inkling of the prince he had once been and could become again. And when she did, he was transformed into his beautiful best—not before.

Not only did Christ love me when I was (by his righteous standards) quite unlovely, he loved me enough to die for me so that I could become (again by his standards) altogether beautiful. Just thinking of it makes me feel like waltzing to a song as old as rhyme . . . held fast by the One who romanced and then rescued me with his strong, pursuing love.

> He who did not spare His own Son, but delivered Him over for us all, how will He not also with Him freely give us all things?
>
> Romans 8:32

Even when we are loved, we don't always feel loved. Imagine yourself in the gaze of one who adores you and would go to any lengths to make you his. How good is that?

Dependence Day

I have an idea for a new national holiday . . . an observance of a principle so key to human joy and satisfaction that I'm amazed no one has yet suggested it. My holiday would be called "Dependence Day," and it would be celebrated 365 days a year, year after year, until time ceases to be measured. Probably the reason no one has suggested Dependence Day before now is that we're celebrators of *independence,* not dependence. But we are meant to rely completely on the One who loves us like no other!

In Hosea 13, God says to Israel: "You were not to know any god except Me, for there is no savior besides Me" (v. 4). God illustrates his pursuit of his wayward people through the life of husband/prophet Hosea, who pursued, married, was deserted by, and then rescued a faithless prostitute named Gomer.

Hosea pursued Gomer-gone-bad for the same purpose God pursued Israel: he meant to do her good. He means to do us good too. If we believed this, we'd be lining up to surrender to God's pursuit, but instead we run from him, because we value our independence more than we relish his care. We long for freedom from authority more than we long for protection from harm. We're more comfortable with self-sufficiency than we are with surrender. And the end to our arrogance is not good: "It is your destruction, O Israel, that you are against Me, against your help" (Hos. 13:9).

So how do we go about declaring Dependence Day? Hosea instructs us there too: "Return, O Israel, to the LORD your God, for you have stumbled because of your iniquity. Take words with you and return to the LORD . . ." (14:1–2).

What kind of words? Words like "I've stumbled." Words like "you're my only hope." Words that confess all others have failed us. Words of thanks for his freshness and beauty and strength . . . words that might sound something like this:

"God, I *do* depend on you for everything, even my next breath. I cannot do one thing without you. You provided a way for me to know you by sending your precious Son Jesus to die. You give grace for living the Christ-life too and keep right on forgiving and cleansing me. You are my hope, my strength, my security, my song, my hiding place, my rock, my fortress, my defender, my friend, and the truest lover of my soul. Today I declare Dependence Day. I renounce my prideful, pretend-independence, and confess my overwhelming need for you. Help me to cease striving and know that you are indeed God—and I most certainly am not. In Jesus's holy name . . . amen."

"For she does not know that it was I who gave her the grain, the new wine and the oil, and lavished on her silver and gold."

Hosea 2:8

In his excellent book The Pleasures of God, *John Piper writes: "God is like a highway patrolman pursuing you down the interstate with lights flashing and siren blaring to get you to stop—not to give you a ticket, but to give you a message so good it couldn't wait till you get home."[2] There is no risk in surrender. He means to do you good, always.*

This Is My Father's World

I love hymns. Old familiar ones like "Amazing Grace" and "The Old Rugged Cross" and "Standing on the Promises," and less-frequently sung ones like "O Sacred Head Now Wounded" and "Sometimes a Light Surprises" and "Be Thou My Vision." I learned hymns, tens and then hundreds of them, the easy way—hearing them over and over, Sunday after Sunday—beginning before I could actually comprehend their meaning, when I was small enough to rest my chin on the pew in front of me as I stood with the grown-ups to sing.

The first hymn I memorized (including the obscure third verse that Baptists, for some mysterious reason, rarely sung) was "This Is My Father's World." I memorized it not because it was assigned to me and the other kids in the children's choir of the First Baptist Church of Portland, Texas, but because its words and melody ambushed my heart and moved in to take permanent residence. I am glad for that.

I'm glad because when I see a brilliant pink and purple sky in the moments just before dusk, I hear "This is my Father's world: I rest me in the thought of rocks and trees and skies and seas; His hand the wonders wrought." And I remember whom to thank for the wonder I've just witnessed. I'm glad because when I think I've heard the slightest whisper from God saying, "Go this way, Leigh" or "trust me here," I'm reminded "in the rustling grass I hear Him pass; He speaks to me everywhere." And I believe that it is his voice I have heard, indeed.

And I'm glad because all is not always well.

Promises are broken. This is my Father's world. Children are hungry. This is my Father's world. Buildings fall. This is my Father's world. Snipers fire. This is my Father's world. Good men fail. This is my Father's world. Dreams are delayed. This is my Father's world.

I know, of course, that the Word of God contains all the truth I need pertaining to life and godliness in this broken and beautiful world. But it's the music that helps me remember that "The earth is the LORD's, and all it contains, the world, and those who dwell in it" (Ps. 24:1). The Presbyterian minister in upstate New York who wrote the words to this particular hymn that I love drew his inspiration from frequent walks he took in the woods near his home. Starting out each time, he would say to anyone who might be near enough to hear: "I'm going out to see my Father's world."

"This is my Father's world, a wanderer I may roam. Whate'er my lot, it matters not, my heart is still at home."

The heavens are telling of the glory of God; and their expanse is declaring the work of His hands. Day to day pours forth speech, and night to night reveals knowledge.

Psalm 19:1–2

204

Sometimes reading the headlines makes me wonder whose world this really is. But the headlines aren't the last word. What do you see and hear that makes you question whether this is our Father's world? What have you seen and heard that makes you sure that it is?

Love beyond Degree

I'm a nut for poetry. I have favorites. Emily Dickinson. John Donne. Shakespeare. Gerard Manley Hopkins. Christina Rossetti and the Brownings, both Robert and Elizabeth. But there's one classic sonnet I believe totally missed the mark. It begins like this: "How do I love thee? Let me count the ways. . . ."

Stop!

If you love me, really love me, can you ever hope to *count*? Because counting is finite, and the love I believe each of us hungers for is . . . well . . . infinite. It can't be tallied like a score sheet or balanced like a bank account. If it can, it's not big enough.

Although Elizabeth Barrett Browning's XLIII of *Sonnets from the Portugese* is beautiful, and even hints at a human love that transcends death, I'm sad when the last line is punctuated with a period. That's it? That's all? Call me a glutton, but I wanted more.

When my nieces were small, my sister and brother-in-law heard their prayers and put them to bed each night with these words: "We love you more than the oceans." That gets closer to it, I think. It says, "We love you more than the biggest thing we can think of, more than we could ever hope to measure."

That beats Browning in my book . . . but still there's more.

That "more" is not the story of imperfect man loving in a way that mimics perfection. It's the story of perfect God loving imperfect man enough to *make him* perfect. Paul writes, "For while we were still helpless, at the right time Christ died for the ungodly. For one will hardly die for a righteous man; though perhaps for the good man someone would dare even to die. But God demonstrates His own love toward us, in that while we were yet sinners, Christ died for us" (Rom. 5:6–8).

And from the apostle John: "In this is love, not that we loved God, but that He loved us and sent His Son to be the propitiation for our sins" (1 John 4:10).

One evening a few weeks before Christmas, I flipped on the radio on my way home from work and heard an amazing voice. The voice belonged to Jubilant Sykes, and as the NPR reporter interviewed him, I was so spellbound that I didn't go straight home. I couldn't. I detoured to my neighborhood Barnes and Noble and bought the only two CDs in the store with his name on them. One was a collection of pop standards, and the other was a gospel recording.

I've heard one of the songs in my newfound "Jubilant" collection all my life, but in his soaring baritone I was rendered breathless by a phrase I'd never paid much attention to before. You'll have to settle here for just the words: "Was it for sins that I had done He groaned upon the tree? Amazing pity, grace unknown, and love . . . beyond . . . degree."

Love beyond degree. Praise God. He didn't—and he doesn't— count the ways.

> The Lord appeared to him from afar, saying, "I have loved you with an everlasting love; therefore I have drawn you with lovingkindness."
>
> Jeremiah 31:3

It sounds romantic to hear someone "count the ways" that you are loved. But what if those things changed? What if they were never even true to begin with? How much more wonderful it is to be loved in spite of, not because of—and to know that nothing can change the mind of the Giver of that love! You and I are loved with a "love beyond degree."

The Determined Hound of Heaven

*O*f all the bad break-up lines I've heard (and I have surely sampled my fair share) the worst/best of all had to be this one: "I'm like the dog that chased the car and caught it. I don't know what to do with you." The analogy, while most unwelcome at the time, was absolutely dead-on. I couldn't have said it better myself.

Dogs don't chase cars to catch them. They chase cars for the sheer exhilaration of chasing cars. This particular "chaser," never imagining he might actually catch the object of his pursuit, had given little thought to what he might do if—and when—that happened.

Once his quarry stopped running for good, he quickly lost interest, or courage, or both.

God is a different kind of chaser. He's the hound of heaven that, once he sets his sights on us, pursues not only with passion, but with purpose. He knows the plans he has for us. He never loses sight of them. He means to overtake and then overwhelm us with his persistent love. And he's never disappointed or frightened or confused when we stop running. He's delighted. He pursues with unwavering intent, knowing just what to do with each of us at the end of the chase.

He knows what to do with our sin. "If we confess our sins, He is faithful and righteous to forgive us our sins and to cleanse us from all unrighteousness" (1 John 1:9).

He knows what to do with our tears. "You have taken account of my wanderings; put my tears in Your bottle; are they not in Your book?" (Ps. 56:8).

He knows what to do with the gifts he has given us. "For we are His workmanship, created in Christ Jesus for good works, which God prepared beforehand so that we would walk in them" (Eph. 2:10).

He knows what to do with our empty places. "That He would grant you, according to the riches of His glory, to be strengthened with power through His Spirit in the inner man, so that Christ may dwell in your hearts through faith" (Eph. 3:16–17a).

Have you heard the unmistakable breathing of the heavenly hound? Has he kept pace with you, whether you've sped up, or slowed down, or hidden in the shadows hoping he might simply pass you by? He will not. He is relentless. The love he means to bestow on the object of his chase is boundless—and he never hesitates. Not only because he loves the chase, but because he means to share with us forever the unimaginable joy of being caught.

Listen. Can you hear your pursuer? Every nearing footfall bears his message: You are loved. You are loved. You are loved. You are loved. The precious hound of heaven is ever at your heels.

"They shall be My people, and I will be their God; and I will give them one heart and one way, that they may fear Me always, for their own good and for the good of their children after them. I will make an everlasting covenant with them that I will not turn away from them, to do them good; and I will put the fear of Me in their hearts so that they will not turn away from Me. I will rejoice over them to do them good and will faithfully plant them in this land with all My heart and with all My soul."

Jeremiah 32:38–41

God's not chasing you for the fun of it. He means for you to be held fast in his enduring embrace. Are you running today? What if you simply stopped and let yourself be caught?

"I See the Moon"

*E*very night before bedtime when we were small, my sister and I said our "God blesses" with our parents close by. "I see the moon and the moon sees me," we'd begin together, "God bless the moon and God bless me." Then we'd leave the moon for still more distant lights: "I see the stars and the stars see me, God bless the stars and God bless me."

Our "God blesses" started big (the heavens!) then got sweetly small as one by one we'd name every member of our extended family—grandparents, aunts, uncles, and cousins—and ask God to bless them too. It was the surest liturgy of my childhood, and I can't remember more than a handful of nights that it was missed.

I don't say my "God blesses" anymore. My prayers these days are less scheduled and a lot more complex. But they're not any more profound or true. Those childhood prayers were the alphabet that taught me to piece together prayer's language, and although I add more words today, the subject/verb/object structure of yesterday is still at the very heart of it all.

God is, and should be, the subject of my devotion, the recipient of my requests, and the acknowledged One who blesses all that is (and who are) blessed. It's just that simple. Even now. So when my mind is jumbled or my heart is troubled, when I can't find the words to order my grown-up prayers to God, I'm thinking that "I see the moon . . ." might not be a bad way to start.

Oh, I know the *moon* doesn't really see me. But the moon-Maker does. Tonight his moon is waning just a shade past full, and as it sits low and golden in the autumn sky I plan to whisper, "I see the moon and the moon sees me, God bless the moon and God bless me." Then, because he really *is* the One who sees us all and holds within himself the power to bless us, I'm going to name as many names as I can call to mind, and ask him to do just that.

Maybe I'll even be saying yours.

May the LORD answer you in the day of trouble! May the name of the God of Jacob set you securely on high! May He send you help from the sanctuary and support you from Zion! May He remember all your meal offerings and find your burnt offering acceptable! May He grant you your heart's desire and fulfill all your counsel! We will sing for joy over your victory, and in the name of our God we will set up our banners. May the LORD fulfill all your petitions . . . Save, O LORD; may the King answer us in the day we call.

Psalm 20:1–5, 9

If the whole concept of prayer seems difficult and overwhelming, why not start small? Aim for an inauspicious beginning . . . but aim to begin. Writer Madeleine L'Engle once advised in a workshop on writing, "Don't be afraid to begin badly. The important thing is to just begin." Her advice probably freed every writer in the room. But maybe it could free some perfectionist "pray-ers" too.

"He's Just *That* Into You"

Probably because I write for a living, I'm fascinated by those books that seem to capture enough of a commanding audience to become tout-able "bestsellers." Good writing, I've discovered, is not enough. (Sometimes good writing is not even a requirement!) One word from Oprah can make a book a bestseller. Strong word of mouth may help, but it won't do the trick alone. Sometimes there's just no telling what will catch the imagination of the reading public and run away with it.

Who would have thought a book for lovesick women called *He's Just Not That Into You* would find fame on the self-help charts and be featured for weeks on too many television talk shows to count?

The author of *He's Just Not That Into You* is not a counselor, a psychologist, or a sociologist. He's not any particular sort of relationship expert at all. He's just a thirty-something guy who thinks he's discovered the one thing about men that every woman should know. (How's *that* for a delicious premise?) What's that one thing? Where a man's feelings are concerned, his actions speak louder than words. Always. And you know what? I think the book resonated so strongly because, way down deep, women know he's telling them the truth.

Maybe that's why the daughter of Herod asked for John the Baptist's head on a plate, or princesses asked their would-be princes to slay dragons or swim moats, or an exasperated

Eliza Doolittle pleaded with fumbling Freddy to stop talking and "Show me!"

Action is, after all, a pretty accurate measure of interest. If someone is "into you," you're going to know it. You won't have to guess. I learned that lesson long before what's-his-name wrote *He's Just Not That Into You*. I learned it from a nonfiction bestseller too, but not his. I learned it from the positive view, not the negative one. And I learned it about an everlasting love, not a temporal one.

Here's how action proved to me that I am loved, and this is only the tiniest sample.

And the Word became flesh, and dwelt among us, and we beheld His glory.

John 1:14

As He was going along by the Sea of Galilee, He saw Simon and Andrew, the brother of Simon, casting a net in the sea; for they were fishermen. And Jesus said to them, "Follow Me, and I will make you become fishers of men."

Mark 1:16-17 NASB

[Jesus] rose from supper, and laid aside His garments; and taking a towel . . . began to wash the disciples' feet, and to wipe them with the towel with which He was girded.

John 13:4–5

And the chief priests accused Him of many things, but He answered nothing.

Mark 15:3 NKJ

And when they came to the place called The Skull, there they crucified Him . . . but Jesus was saying,

"Father, forgive them; for they do not know what they are doing."

Luke 23:33–34

And Jesus uttered a loud cry, and breathed His last.

Mark 15:37

It seems too good to be true, doesn't it—that Someone would love you that much? But actions really *do* speak louder than words. Believe it. He's just THAT into you.

For God so loved the world, that He gave His only begotten Son, that whoever believes in Him should not perish, but have eternal life.

John 3:16

In the end, love is something you do. And everything that Jesus did was a testimony of his love for you and me. Without using words, tell someone today how much you love them. Without using words, tell Jesus too.

From the Mouths of Rock Stars

My taste in reading could be politely called eclectic, or more critically challenged as a tiny bit schizophrenic. I'm all over the map. During any given week I'm likely to have several books "going" at once. Between my desk, the night table by my bed, and the living room ottoman, the present inventory includes a two-pound biography of Pope John Paul II, a novel about the Sudan, another Pulitzer-winning novel I'm re-reading slowly because it was so delicious the first time, a stack of miscellaneous news and decorating magazines, and an old Nancy Drew book. (Seriously. I would not kid about Nancy.)

But the book that keeps moving with me from room to room these days is titled simply *Bono*. It's a rambling, Q&A interview of Irish U2 rocker Paul Hewson, known for decades by a single moniker, and it's a fascinating read.

Bono is a man of many titles—singer, songwriter, political activist, believer, husband, father, rock star. His words are alternately insightful, irritating, humble, self-attuned and, most often, arresting. I've found myself scribbling down phrases and bits of paragraphs on whatever's nearby, wanting to think more on them later.

While his interviewer prods him frequently to describe the relief work he and his wife, Ali, have done in Ethiopia, he's mostly reticent about the details. But one particularly descriptive passage caught me: "The camp was about feeding, but myself and Ali were in charge of the orphanage. We slept in a tent. In the morning, as the mist would lift, we would see thousands of people walking in lines toward the camp, people who had been walking for great distances through the night—men, women, children, families who'd lost everything, taking a few possessions on a voyage to meet mercy."[3]

It was those last few words that stopped me cold: "Taking a few possessions on a voyage to meet mercy." This was the rock star's description of the hungry, impoverished people he saw making their way to the African camp in hopes of receiving food. But to me, it was a worthy description of what I'd like my life to be.

It's not about storing up stuff. It can't be—because you really *can't* take it with you. This time I, you, we, have here is not all there is, and it's both more—and less—than what it's cracked up to be. This life really *is* a journey to somewhere else, and we make it expectantly, hungry, and more full of hope than of anything. If we make it well, we won't be carrying much. We can't, and expect to travel far.

If someone asks me what it is I'm about, I'd like to be able to truthfully say, "I'm taking a few possessions on a voyage to meet mercy." And I'd like for that to be so true that saying it would be redundant. Only, in my version of the rock star's epigram, I'd mean to take others along with me on the voyage, and my "mercy" would have a capital "M." You and I would call him Jesus.

> If anyone wishes to come after Me, he must deny himself, and take up his cross daily and follow Me.
>
> Luke 9:23

What are you carrying with you on your voyage to meet Mercy? Is it enabling you to travel well or slowing you down so that you're hardly moving at all?

Of Football and Messiahs

I typically miss the Super Bowl, a fact I don't much regret. It's hard for me to get excited about this over-hyped event, or any football game for that matter, that doesn't involve the Fightin' Texas Aggies, or any boys I know under the age of twelve.

Even when I miss the big game, though, I almost always read about it in the next morning's paper. And after the 2003 Super Bowl I discovered that apparently football has become something more than mere sport—at least to some. This postgame quote by the winning Tampa Bay owner, about the winning Tampa Bay coach, struck me as very odd indeed: "He came from heaven, and he took us to heaven." (The second aforementioned heaven, presumably, being a winning locker room; the first, California.)

Wow. He came from heaven, and he took us to heaven. And "he" was a football coach! Last time I checked, the Messiah spot was more than ably occupied.

Honestly, I'm not sure if I'm more repelled by this statement or intrigued. Repelled because it ascribes holiness to an NFL coach, and intrigued because it uses the language of eternal deliverance to express a fleeting, earthly high. Are we so starved for a taste of heaven that a blowout of a ballgame will do it for us? Some of us might be. And that's sobering.

When modern men and women buy more than they need, eat more than they want, drink more than they should, and risk more than they ought—just what is it they really want? What do most ordinary people—along with extreme skiers, stock market shamans, surgically enhanced starlets, and public power brokers—have in common?

They all want more. And they don't have a clue what that "more" might be, because they are seldom looking beyond the moment, or beyond themselves.

In his wonderful book *Orthodoxy*, G. K. Chesterton wrote, "That Jones shall worship the god within him turns out ultimately to mean that Jones shall worship Jones. Let Jones worship the sun or moon, anything other than the Inner Light; let Jones worship cats or crocodiles, if he can find any in his street, but not the god within. Christianity came into the world firstly in order to assert with violence that a man had not only to look inwards, but to look outwards, to behold with astonishment and enthusiasm a divine company and a divine captain."[4]

"A divine company and a divine captain." That's what we long for, whether we know it or not. And all the winning coaches in the world can't help us there. We can't even help ourselves.

We need the real thing. The Messiah who really *did* come from heaven and really *can* take us there. His name is Jesus. Sorry, Coach Gruden. No lesser deliverer will do.

In Him we have redemption through His blood, the forgiveness of our trespasses, according to the riches of His grace which He lavished on us.

Ephesians 1:7–8

With my words I sometimes ascribe honor and glory where it does not belong. I confess that I am not always careful with language—and I love it dearly. May God guard my lips today and keep me from speaking thoughtlessly about the things that matter most.

Only Words

*I*n my house full of books, I noticed two lying very near one another: *Haven*, a decorating book by Chris Madden, and *Heaven*, a theology book by Randy Alcorn. Only one letter separates the two titles. Just a single, lowercase "e" sets them apart, but that one letter spans time and eternity. *Haven* instructs me how to feather my earthly nest in a way that satisfies, nurtures, and fulfills, and *heaven* reports that my earthly nest is temporary and meager at best, compared to the indescribable glory that is to come.

One single letter of one single word bridges the entire expanse of what is and is to come. A single letter interrupts a string of others to remind me how much words matter. And they do. "The mind—" says writer Annie Dillard, "the culture—has two little tools, grammar and lexicon: a decorated sand bucket and a matching shovel. With these we bluster about the continents and do all the world's work. With these we try to save our very lives."[5]

I couldn't begin to add up the number of words I read, write, hear, or simply absorb unconsciously in any given day. I'm certain that it's in the thousands—perhaps tens of thousands, or even hundreds, maybe. My word processing software has a handy feature called "Word Count" that tells me how many I've created by keystroke, but not how many I've considered and rejected because they weren't quite right. There's simply no counting them all. To do so would require that I stop living and do nothing more than add.

Because I'm often intoxicated by words and combinations of words, I marvel at this: God spoke, and the Word—all that he is—became flesh. The story he had written out of time came into time and unfolded before the very eyes of its audience. The Word became flesh, and the story came to life. With one Word—Jesus—God-the-author embodied redemption and revelation all at once and for always. With one Word he pierced the darkness, paid the ransom, split the veil, and ran toward the prodigal on his dusty, desperate road home.

Just a single word.

When I was a little girl, my sister practiced the piano daily in our neat-as-a-pin living room. She played her assigned songs, but others too—out of a more contemporary songbook. My favorite one to hear was an old BeeGees song called simply "Words." And the lyrics that accompanied the last few notes were the ones that I loved best, even before I knew why: "It's only words, and words are all I have, to take your heart away." May it ever be so.

And the Word became flesh and dwelt among us, and we beheld His glory, the glory as of the only begotten of the Father, full of grace and truth . . . and of His fullness we have all received, and grace for grace.

John 1:14,16

Singer/songwriter/author Michael Card, in his wonderful song "The Final Word," said, "God spoke the incarnation

and then so was born the Son; His final word was Jesus
—He needed no other one." That final word is the very
Word that has stolen my heart away.

"It's about the Movie"

I was having a delightful dinner with my friend Scott.
My smart, ambitious, utterly competent, and very success-
ful friend Scott. He and his beautiful wife embody a perfect
power couple with heart: they are strong and lovely inside
and out. He had come to town on business, and we made
plans to meet before his flight home. In the middle of a
crowded Italian restaurant, plates and glasses clinking,
waiters bustling and conversation at a low roar, we caught
one another up on what God is doing in our lives. Dinner
lasted three hours and we'd barely scratched the surface.

I've known Scott for more years than either of us would
comfortably admit. He lurked in the back of my Bible study
class way back when and routinely offered encouraging and
enthusiastic feedback on each week's lesson. One day we
went to lunch after church, and it quickly became apparent
that God had chosen for me a friend for life.

Both of us, in different ways, have managed to deflect
the full weight of God's head-on and highly personal call
for a good long while. We may have done it in different
ways, but the result has been the same: a dull dissatisfaction
with even the very best things we could get for ourselves.
But lately, my friend and I have relaxed our grip on the
wheel and seen amazing stuff happen. Things we didn't
engineer. Things we can't control. Things that have caused
us to shake our heads in wonder. Because when God says,
"Follow me," he means just that. And sometimes that's all

the information we get. The next move is clearly his. Our job is to fall in behind him in obedient belief.

Somewhere between the veal and the tiramisu, my dear friend looked at me and said: "You get this, right? It's not about the money. It's not about the deal. It's about the *movie*. Are you watching?"

I'm watching, Scott. And this time my eyes aren't fixed on the end of the road. They're on the small patch of ground my sweet Savior's feet just left. I'm matching my steps to his and trying not to miss a thing as this marvelous movie called capital-L *Life* unfolds, frame by glorious frame.

> "But he who enters by the door is a shepherd of the sheep. To him the doorkeeper opens, and the sheep hear his voice, and he calls his own sheep by name and leads them out. When he puts forth all his own, he goes ahead of them, and the sheep follow him because they know his voice. . . . I am the door; if anyone enters through Me, he will be saved, and will go in and out and find pasture. The thief comes only to steal and kill and destroy; I came that they may have life, and have it abundantly."
>
> John 10:2–4, 9–10

Films are made up of scenes, and scenes are made up of movements and dialogue and images combining to tell a story. They unfold a second at a time. Each second informs the next, and the next. I can get ahead of myself in this drama if I'm not careful and miss the significance of the moment. Abundant life isn't only abundant at the end—it's meant to be abundant all along the way.

"Can You Hear Me Now?"

Remember the phone network commercial where a caller with a cellular phone pressed to his ear moves from place to obscure place and asks, "Can you hear me now? Can you hear me now?" Marketing strategists undoubtedly had survey or focus group data to prove that cellular customers value clear and uninterrupted reception, no matter where they're calling from.

How about the one that shows various customers screaming in anguish when they receive their (unexpectedly high) bill? Again—bet there's more data that shows they want reasonable monthly rates with no big surprise surcharges. (And who doesn't?)

All I wanted was voice mail.

I'd been a cell phone user for years, but I seldom left it on to receive calls. I mostly used it for calling out. I figured I was as available to the world-at-large as I wanted to be. But when my hours became more erratic and my office less established, voice mail seemed like a good option to activate. At least until I tried.

Yes, the cellular provider confirmed, I *did* have voice mail on my account. It could be activated using the phone itself and a few simple directions from the network's website. Not so fast, I discovered. The website instructions didn't produce the result I was looking for. So I searched for a "prompt" option that said "contact a Company-x customer service representative." There wasn't one.

I tried calling (with their own phone) the company. *No deal*. I visited a nearby retail location. One hour and fifteen minutes later (with *them* calling their own customer service center), *no deal*. At one point the very young and cheerful employee who was trying to help suggested a trip to the juice bar next door for what he called "a calming smoothie."

When I returned with my smoothie in hand, he shook his head and said, "I've emailed my manager, but I think you should take it to the local service center/super store on Monday and see if they can do it."

So on Monday, I did. And the very nice man who waited on me there went through the same routine without success. I could re-add voice mail for $1.99 a month, he said, and perhaps circumvent the snag. When he heard my exaggerated sigh, he offered to call customer service again. As he stood (on hold) waiting for another rep to answer, it hit me. Pray, silly. Just pray. So silently, I did. And in a matter of seconds (I am *not* kidding) he punched a couple of numbers, smiled, handed me my phone, and said, "You're all set." Then, almost under his breath, he said, "God is so good."

Two days, three hours, one calming smoothie, ten miles, and three service people later, I had prayed. (And I think he might have too.) I'm not sure, but I believe I just heard my Father saying, "Can you hear me now, Leigh? Can you hear me now?"

You bet I can, Lord. Loud and clear.

"Ask, and it will be given to you; seek, and you will find; knock, and it will be opened to you."

Matthew 7:7

Why is it that we neglect to pray? Why will we try everything in our own power before we ask God to intervene for us with his? If there is something you've been grappling with to no avail, it's time to pray.

Embraceable Inconsistencies

I'm neat. Not freakishly, compulsively neat—but orderly. I like things to make sense. It pleases me when one thing logically follows another. Like when the conclusion of a good book somehow affirms its beginning. Or when I intuitively reach for something in the place it should be . . . and it is there.

But while there's comfort in finding things *as* you expected, *where* you expected—there's also something a little thrilling about the odd placements of life. Like the single azalea that bloomed in my hedge more than a month after the thousands of others had faded and fallen. Or opening the newspaper and seeing that the sports section has been completely redesigned. Or discovering that my favorite neighborhood coffee shop has stopped making pistachio muffins and has begun experimenting with cranberries.

Just when you think you've got the story . . . when the routine becomes sweetly ordinary, God seems to specialize in changing things. In shaking up the mix a bit. In a movie review I read recently, one of the actors was asked if the audience was meant to "like" his character—whether he was meant to be a "good" person or a "bad" one. He replied, "As an actor, I have always felt there is a risk in trying to reconcile everything about a character. You must *embrace the inconsistencies*."

That last phrase intrigued me enough to tear out the paragraph surrounding it, and leave the scrap of newsprint on my bedside table for later pondering.

Embrace the inconsistencies.

Do you suppose a road closing could be an embraceable inconsistency? Or a harsh word from a normally gentle friend? What about a snowstorm in April, or a last-minute gate change at the airport?

And if I could learn to embrace the smaller, relatively painless inconsistencies in life, do you suppose I could ever learn to love the larger ones—so that, like the apostle Paul I might one day say, "We have this treasure in jars of clay to show that this all-surpassing power is from God and not from us . . . always carry[ing] around in our body the death of Jesus, so that the life of Jesus may also be revealed" (2 Cor. 4:7, 10 NIV).

Maybe so. I hope so.

I'd like to embrace weakness so that strength can be showcased. I'd like to embrace emptiness so that fullness might be wildly celebrated.

I'd like to because I'm the beneficiary of one of the most illogical, unpredictable, unexpected inconsistencies of all: "The people walking in darkness have seen a great light; on those living in the land of the shadow of death a light has dawned" (Isa. 9:2 NIV). And, "As for you, you were dead in your transgressions and sins . . . but because of his great love for us, God, who is rich in mercy, made us alive with Christ" (Eph. 2:1, 4 NIV).

That's an inconsistency I can't hope to get my arms around. But I'm not about to stop trying.

My nature is to seek to resolve inconsistency, not embrace it. The idea of drawing confusion close is not so very comforting. But the kingdom of heaven is a kingdom of beautiful paradox. And at the heart of it lies the most surprising one of all.

God in the Details

"God is in the details" is a phrase I've heard plenty of times—enough to cause me to wonder who first said it, and why. So I spent some time recently searching for the source of this particular phrase (you may justly call me a word-nerd) and discovered that it's a knock-off of sorts.

The original epigram was "the *devil* is in the details," meant to convey that even the grandest projects may be sabotaged in their smallest components. Maybe so, but I like the God-version better.

It's attributed to Le Corbusier, a twentieth-century French architect and city planner—a man known for designing buildings with unusual curves and unconventional shapes. Maybe he sat at his drawing table one day and decided he was weary of sketching structural box after structural box and wondered what would happen if he softened just a corner or two, here and there. And maybe the result of his noodling was delight, so he did it again and kept on doing it.

I acknowledge God often as the architect of the Grand Design—but I also frequently fail to give him praise as the God of the small and intricate. He's not only the God who spoke worlds into being, divided seas, defeated armies, and once and for all plundered the grave—he's the God who invaded history and time in the form of an embryo, invented eyelashes, saves my tears in a bottle, and decided one thousand shades of green weren't near enough, and so made a few thousand more.

How can I not love a God who so loves the details?

And because he *is* in the details of this world, shouldn't he also be manifest in the details of my life? Couldn't he be recognized in a hug that lasts half a second longer than it might, or a word swallowed that rises up in indignation when I think I have been wronged?

Isn't he exalted in the decision of my artist-friend who remixes a color she's already placed on the linen canvas before her because it doesn't yet match the one she sees in her mind's eye? And doesn't he shine in the silence of my counselor friend who waits another second or two for a response he knows is struggling to make its way out of his client's heart? And couldn't he be in the patience of a tired mother of two, who uses a cookie cutter to make a peanut butter sandwich look like a dinosaur when a butter knife would do just as well?

Oh, yes. My God is definitely in the details. I am more decided than ever to remain on the lookout for them.

> "Yours, O LORD, is the greatness and the power and the glory and the victory and the majesty, indeed everything that is in the heavens and the earth; Yours is the dominion, O LORD, and You exalt Yourself as head over all." 1 Chronicles 29:11

Poet Gerard Manley Hopkins wrote, "Christ plays in ten thousand places,/ Lovely in limbs, and lovely in eyes not his/To the Father through the features of men's faces." Can you spy out a few of those places where the Son of God is at play?

God Is Love

Someone had lettered the white pressboard sign by hand with a red magic marker and posted it on a busy street corner. As I pulled up to the light and traffic whizzed past,

I glanced out my window and saw it propped up jauntily near the curb: "God is love," it said. That's all.

No sales pitch. No phone number, or discount offer, or invitation to visit www. anything. Just "God is love."

It was the last day of an eventful year. (And my birthday to boot.) I was on my way to a nail appointment and feeling slightly flu-ish, distracted by my own coughing and feeling every bit of another year older. But when I saw the sign I had to smile. "He is," I agreed out loud with its anonymous creator. "He is indeed *that*."

I don't know what prompted the sign's maker to leave it in front of a strip center at a high-traffic intersection . . . or what it might have accomplished while it was temporarily on display there. To me it was a reminder of a truth I've known for a long time but can never hear enough—the Lord of the universe, the Maker of all that is, is the one thing we want more than almost anything else, and he is love.

Only, not cheap love. Or flimsy love. Or fleeting love. No, he's the kind of long-suffering, deliberate, full-on, full-out love that scares you to death before it delivers you. The kind that means business and doesn't bluff or blink or fool around. He is the kind of love that dies to redeem its beloved and then kicks death in the teeth to make it stick. And any reminder of that, even a hastily scrawled and randomly placed one, is a welcome reminder.

Because he *is* love, love is within my reach. Nearer than my next breath. More sure than the sunrise. Because he *is* love, I have a go-by for loving. I've seen defining love, and I have a pattern to follow. Because he *is* love, love is not a mere vapor, or a feeling, or an idea.

Because he *is* love, love has a name—and it's one that I know: Jesus.

God is love. When we take up permanent residence in a life of love, we live in God and God lives in us. This way, love has the run of the house, becomes at home and mature in us, so that we're free of worry on Judgment Day—our standing in the world is identical with Christ's. There is no room in love for fear. Well-formed love banishes fear. . . . First we were loved, now we love. He loved us first.

1 John 4:17–19 Message

What would change in your life today if you believed—and acted on—the truth that God is love?

"The Good Kind of Cry"

An email from a well-spoken friend contained this phrase I couldn't stop turning over in my head. She referred to someone she loved crying "the good kind of cry," and I felt instinctively what those few simple words conveyed. Some tears are so unbidden, and pure, and necessary that they cleanse and heal, almost without us. Such tears are the essential lubricant for that "good kind of cry" my friend described.

They can't be conjured any more than they can be quieted. They simply *are*, for as long as they need to be. They aren't manipulative, or especially dramatic, or perhaps even readily visible. But these tears can speak volumes when words won't do at all. And they can respond with powerful eloquence when the muscles of our faces or arms or legs are rendered frozen and still.

The good kind of cry is called out by purest beauty . . . or heartbreak . . . or joy . . . or unfettered worship. *Old Yeller* may have been my first experience of it (pure heartbreak), but the good kind of cry surprised me again just recently when a classically trained opera singer rendered a simple song called "Lamb of God" in my inner-city church's morning worship service. The notes she hit and held bypassed rational thought and pierced my heart before I could defend myself. It was definitely "the good kind of cry."

The good kind of cry has ambushed me as I've stood before paintings in the Museé d'Orsay, and as I've watched a newborn baby's jerky hands and feet move out of rhythm, punching air. Tears have washed my face more than once when a gold, round moon has hung low in the nighttime sky, and when I've been surprised by a sudden, small hint of the big-time love of God.

I used to be ashamed of the "good kind of cry" tears, but I'm not so much anymore. Sometimes I don't even bother to wipe them away. I just let them fall. And when I do, I remember this verse that I stumbled on years ago, and still love just as much as I did when I first read it: "You have taken account of my wanderings; put my tears in Your bottle; are they not in Your book?" (Ps. 56:8). I don't have to catch them. They're precious to the One who calls them forth, and he saves each one.

> And standing behind Him at His feet, weeping, she began to wet His feet with her tears, and kept wiping them with the hair of her head, and kissing His feet, and anointing them with the perfume.
>
> Luke 7:38

The next time unbidden tears well up in you — don't fight it. Go ahead. Have "the good kind of cry." It's an altogether fitting thing to do.

When the Answer Is "No"

*F*unny thing about "no": it never gets any easier to hear. I wasn't fond of it when I was seven, or eleven, or twenty-one. And I don't like it one bit better today. I learned early on to ask politely, and to order my request to the one who was most able (and likely) to grant it. I said, "May I, please," and I said it to the parent I thought might answer "yes." I learned there's a fine line between persistence and annoyance. And I walked it like a tightrope.

It feels like I've been hearing "no" a lot lately. Like the departing jokers who removed the "w" keys from White House computers four years ago, if I didn't know better, I'd think vandals had stripped God's messaging system of its "y's"—because his "yes's" have been fewer and farther between.

I don't believe my requests have been unreasonable or even selfish as far as I've been able to discern. And I've asked respectfully and as often as I dare. I've offered up to God what Spurgeon called "order and argument" in prayer, and I've prayed believing that the things I've asked are well within his power. I still believe it.

And I'm still hearing "no."

When I heard it over and over as a kid, I eventually relented. I moved on. I abandoned my unmet requests and began to focus my desires elsewhere. (And sometimes I even gave the one who delivered the "no" the cold shoulder for a while.)

That doesn't work anymore. There are some desires that, for whatever reason, you simply cannot abandon, even when holding on to them hurts more than ditching them might. And the One who hears my requests these days cannot be easily abandoned or ignored. I need him too much and love him too deeply for that. Even when he tells me no, it's him I want, him I trust, him I bring my wants and hopes and needs to. Because whether the answer is yes or it's no, he is the One I want to hear it from.

In case you're wondering, I'm still asking. And unless or until you hear otherwise from him, I think you should be too.

> Ask, and it will be given to you; seek, and you will find; knock, and it will be opened to you. For everyone who asks receives, and he who seeks finds, and to him who knocks it will be opened. Or what man is there among you, when his son asks for a loaf, will give him a stone? Or if he asks for a fish, he will not give him a snake, will he? If you then, being evil, know how to give good gifts to your children, how much more will your Father who is in heaven give what is good to those who ask Him!
>
> Matthew 7:7–11

If hearing "no" has you discouraged, take heart. The apostle Paul heard it. So did Jesus. "No" is not a sign of coldness. In fact, it may just be the closest thing to love you've ever known.

The Three That Count

*O*n about rep eleven of a set of fifteen exquisitely de-signed tortures devised by my half-my-age-but-twice-as-buff trainer, I was struggling. He noticed. (He always does.) My arms were beginning to wobble a little, and I couldn't see it, but I'm pretty sure my face was red.

"Come on," he said, "breathe. Push through. *It's the last three that count.*"

231

These are just the sort of words you should never say to someone who "does words" for a living and is in quite enough pain to be a smart aleck. I immediately found the breath to say, "If only the last three count, let's just skip the first twelve."

He laughed . . . and I did four more. When I finished the set, he said this: "You do the first twelve to get to the three that really count. So you need them all." I think he may be too smart for his own good.

For the rest of that day (and a couple more) I've been thinking about those last three reps and his simple words. He's a kinesiology student, so I'm sure he could explain in more detail than I would care to listen to just *why* that "last three" premise is so. But I'm a student of a different kind, so my mind went to another place altogether.

I thought about my Savior, who lived thirty years of relatively ordinary existence before he embarked on the three years that made the history books. Then I thought of the last few days of his thirty-third year and the final Friday, Saturday, and Sunday that changed the world forever. They were grand. Glorious. Necessary! But without all that came before, meaningless.

We tend to think of life in terms of attainment—but I'm beginning to think it's mostly preparation. And that faithfully doing whatever is required of us before "the three that count" is huge. Moses lived some pretty mundane years on the backside of his father-in-law's farm before he got the big job. Those years were preparation. Joseph languished in prison as an innocent man for quite some time before his meteoric rise to power. Every day in his lonely cell was preparation. They didn't know when "the three that count" were coming—or even if they would come. But the "meantime" was making them ready.

I can't say how this applies to you. I can only examine how it applies to me. But I can tell you this: even when they hurt, I'm less and less motivated now to skip the reps that come before "the three that count."

> When all kinds of trials and temptations crowd into your lives, my brothers, don't resent them as intruders, but welcome them as friends! Realize that they come to test your faith and to produce in you the quality of endurance. But let the process go on until that endurance is fully developed, and you will find you have become men of mature character with the right sort of independence.

James 1:1–4 Phillips

Repetition strengthens weak muscles and enables them to perform better. Do not grow weary in doing well on the way to "the three that count."

Worlds Away

good Christmas Devotion

There is no frigate like a book," a poet has said, "to take us worlds away." Books have been my favorite mode of travel since I could tie my own shoes. They've carried me to more places than I can begin to name—from Oz to Narnia and home again, through caves and forests and bogs and even wrinkles in time. I followed a dog named Joe through trials so terrible I thought my heart would break, and held my breath for a pig named Wilbur while his eight-legged friend Charlotte spun her lifesaving web. I wished for Trixie Belden to move to my street and invite me to join the Bobwhites, and for grown-up Nancy Drew to give me a ride in her little red convertible. I imagined a world where all the animals spoke, like my friends in *The*

Wind in the Willows, or where words always rhymed in the trippy, delightful cadence of Dr. Seuss.

Of all the books I've known and loved since childhood, one has carried me farther than all the others combined: the Holy Bible. Its stories and characters are the ones most deeply ingrained in memory: Jonah swallowed up by the great fish, and Noah, building an ark and floating above the mountain peaks in it. Baby Moses, found in the bulrushes (what in the world were those?) by an Egyptian princess while his sister hid nearby, and shepherd boy David winding his slingshot and slaying a giant.

Then there were the gospel stories—the most magical ones of all!—where water became wine, and fishes and loaves multiplied themselves in the biggest picnic of all time. Where blind men got their sight back and a crippled man was lowered through the roof by his friends—and where the wildest waves imaginable were tamed by a land-loving carpenter.

We had a big "coffee table Bible" that I remember being drawn to, but not for reading. It was the elaborate cover and pictures I adored. My own tiny first Bible with my name in gold embossing was more portable and user-friendly. It had pictures too—a comforting one of the nativity and a dark, brooding, frightening one of three crosses on a hill. I scribbled on that one with a purple crayon while sitting in the pews on Sunday and was promptly stood to my feet by my mother and spanked for it.

But while my other books did indeed take me "worlds away"—it was only the Bible that brought its main character smack into my own world.

The Word became flesh and blood, and moved into the neighborhood. We saw the glory with our own eyes, the one-of-a-kind glory, like Father, like Son, generous inside and out, true from start to finish. . . . No one has ever seen God, not so much as a glimpse.

234

This one-of-a-kind God Expression, who exists at the very heart of the Father, has made him plain as day

John 1:14, 18 Message

I still love my books . . . but I could care less about going "worlds away." Especially when God has moved heaven and earth to come and dwell in mine.

Sometimes I'll read a great book and wish that its characters could step off the pages and into my living room. How amazing it is that that is exactly what happened when "the Word became flesh."

Weakness before Wonder

Robert McKee teaches would-be screenwriters how to craft stories that Hollywood will buy. He has analyzed hundreds of scripts, incorporating his principles for screenwriting into a bestselling book called *Story*. He preaches plot and characterization with the fervor of an evangelist. And he is convinced he knows what makes for a memorable story on film.

"Human nature," McKee says, "is fundamentally conservative. We seldom do more than we have to, expend any energy we don't have to, take any risks if we don't have to, change if we don't have to."[6] In other words, we like the status quo. Most of us would prefer to keep our highs and lows within easy range of each other. We favor smooth sailing over the awful thrill of a storm.

For this reason, he argues, it takes pressure—and plenty of it—to make the protagonist of any story "a fully-realized, multidimensional and deeply empathetic character." The more powerful the forces against a character, the richer and more fully realized his (or her) story will be.

Weakness helps us appreciate wonder.

I'm not sure where McKee first discovered his principles. But I'm certain of this: God is the ultimate Storyteller. And he knows his stuff.

His redemptive story comes front and center in every holy week. The hero/protagonist is perfect: fully God and fully man . . . sinless . . . loving . . . wise. There is no power that he does not possess, yet he allows himself to be betrayed, beaten, mocked, and mishandled. He suffers unbelievably, and his punishment comes at the hands of the very ones he meant to save.

He was God. And in those awful moments, God became weak. Hoisted heavenward on a crude Roman cross, he let himself be taunted and ridiculed. He *allowed* it. He *embraced* it. The forces against him were enormous . . . and they were not merely human. "It was now about the sixth hour, and darkness fell over the whole land until the ninth hour, because the sun was obscured; and the veil of the temple was torn in two. And Jesus, crying out with a loud voice, said, 'Father, into Your hands I commit my spirit.' Having said this, He breathed His last" (Luke 23:44–46).

But that was not the end of his story. It was merely the weakness before the wonder.

Without those desperate moments when all seemed lost, there would have been no wondrous resurrection morning—no joyful realization that the bitter end was not the end at all but the best beginning imaginable.

"This Jesus God raised up again, to which we are all witnesses. Therefore having been exalted to the right hand of God, and having received from the Father the promise of the Holy Spirit, He has poured forth this which you both see and hear . . . Therefore let all the house of Israel know for certain that God has made Him both Lord and Christ—this Jesus whom you crucified . . . For the promise is for you and your children and for all who are far off, as many as the Lord our God will call to Himself."

Acts 2:32–33, 36, 39

Praise him for the weakness of the cross. Exalt him for the wonder of the empty tomb. His really is the greatest story ever told, isn't it?

Personal Retreat Guide

Introduction

"Pay attention."

I often heard those words while growing up, probably because I really *wasn't* paying attention. I frequently appeared to be "off somewhere," not focused on the task or person or the assignment at hand. I'm convinced many of us today aren't aware of what God is saying and doing around us because we're simply not paying close attention. Either we're preoccupied with the pressing details of life or we've simply tuned out the still, small, persistent voice of heaven.

But God has not stopped speaking.

This personal retreat guide is crafted to help you hear his voice amid the rush and noise of contemporary life. You don't have to head for the hills to retreat—although if you like the hills, maybe you should. You don't have to devote a full month or a week or even a weekend to work through the ideas and exercises here. You can do them at your own pace, over a few days or for a few hours, or even for a few minutes at a time. You can begin with the ones that interest you most, eventually working through them all, or picking only a few.

The important things are to find a place of undistracted quiet and to begin.

Most of us will never become contemplative. It's simply not our nature. But we can become *everyday observers* who are attuned to the presence of God wherever he reveals himself. Here's a hint: he shows up even when we're not "on retreat," or "having a quiet time." He invades grocery lines and football stadiums, cry rooms and cafeterias. He speaks in ways we expect and in ways we do not. You might imagine the search for him to be something like a spiritual "Where's Waldo," or "Dora the Explorer," since his revelations and manner of speech will vary. His character, however, remains the same: holy, other, full of power and beauty, rich in truth and mercy and wisdom and grace.

"The practice of attention," says Belden C. Lane, "is the rarest of gifts because it depends on the harshest of disciplines. So uncommon is it for us to grasp the beauty and mystery of ordinary things that, when we finally do so, it often brings us to the verge of tears. Appalled by our own poverty, we awake in wonder to a splendor of which we had never dreamed."[1] So what do you say? Will you pay attention with me to "the holy in the everyday?"

First Things

Find a place where you will not be disturbed and carve out a reasonable amount of time to spend in God's presence. Maybe you have an hour. That's great! Maybe you've set aside a day or a weekend—even better! Your getaway could be a room in your house or apartment, a retreat house or cabin, a quiet corner of a bookstore, a coffee shop, a sidewalk café, or a lovely park. Just find a spot where you can listen and observe without having to interact with others. Above all, make it a place you are comfortable.

Have something to write with. You may want to jot down notes about what you see, hear, think, and feel. If you have a small Bible, bring it along. For longer personal retreats I recommend these items, a book or two that speaks to your heart, and music. (I'll recommend some of both—you can use them if you like, or choose not to.)

Finally—leave the communication devices at home, or turn them off. That's right. No cell phone, BlackBerry, pager, etc. Really. This is time for you and God, and he doesn't need those things to speak to you.

Exercise 1: Unburdening

Jesus told a story of a man who, upon finding something of great value, sold everything he had to keep it. Matthew 13:44 says, "The kingdom of heaven is like a treasure hidden in a field, which a man found and hid; and from joy over it he goes and sells all that he has, and buys that field."

Read this verse slowly several times. Read it out loud. Read it silently. Ask yourself if God's kingdom is so precious to you that you would be willing to "divest" yourself of everything else to have it.

If it were, what things would you sell so that you might keep the one great treasure you had found?

Connecting with God is more difficult when our arms are full. Read "Living with My Hands Full" (p. 153) and "Where's Your Treasure" (p. 150) in *The Sacred Ordinary*. Picture your own arms full. Name the burdens, commitments, responsibilities, props, and treasures that you carry. Now breathe deeply . . . and imagine handing them over to Jesus one by one. Name each one, then hand it over into his care. Don't stop until your arms are empty.

You might say something like: "Lord Jesus, here is my _____. You know how closely I guard it, and how fearful I am of being without it. But today, I am "checking it" like luggage and handing it over to your care. I'm doing this because *you* are the one treasure I must have, and because I value you above this _____."

When you're done, sit still and empty-handed before God. Ask him to impress upon you how he would have you fill the space that you've just emptied. Then, "Whatever He says to you, do it." (John 2:5)

MORE READING:

Luke 12:22–34

Philippians 3:7–11

A SOUNDTRACK FOR UNBURDENING:

"Just Come In" by Margaret Becker
"A King and a Kingdom" by Derek Webb
"Take My Life and Let It Be" (hymn)
"I Surrender All" (hymn)
"Farthest Shore" by David Wilcox

LORD GOD ALMIGHTY, I ask not to be enrolled among the earthly great and rich, but to be numbered with the spiritually blessed. Make it my present, supreme, persevering concern to obtain those blessings which are spiritual in their nature, eternal in their continuance, satisfying in their possession.[2]

The Valley of Vision

Exercise 2: Listening

I'm still surprised when someone near me (and alone!) begins speaking out loud—and it's usually because they're responding to a distant person whose voice is transmitting into a Bluetooth device I hadn't noticed in his or her ear! They're tuned in . . . and oblivious to everything around them. I'm guilty of this kind of thing myself when I plug in the ear pieces of my iPod and let my music drown out other sounds.

Can you imagine what it would be like to be "wired" to the voice of God? To hear him over and above everything else?

In Psalm 29, read what David had to say about the voice of the Lord. If you have more than one translation of the Bible handy, read it again in a different one. In any translation, David makes the voice of the Lord seem powerful, indeed: "The voice of the LORD makes the deer to calve, and strips the forests bare, and in His temple, everything says 'Glory!'" (v. 9).

Is God's voice clear to you? Is it obvious that he is speaking, or do you confuse his voice among the others that you hear?

Read "Can You Hear Me Now?" (p. 210) and "Sounding Out the Words" (p. 164) in *The Sacred Ordinary*. Not only does God speak to us—he delights to listen as we speak to him! God's Word tells us that he has spoken through a burning bush, a donkey, a disembodied hand writing on a wall, and countless prophets.

Using your Bible as a reference, record as many instances as you can of God speaking. Consider each instance and the similarities and differences among them. Now turn the paper over and list the ways that *you* have heard God speak. Maybe he has spoken to you through a sermon or a piece of music. Or perhaps through a trusted friend or an experience with nature. Keep writing until you can't think of another example.

Then pray these words from the young prophet Samuel: "Speak, for Thy servant is listening" (1 Sam. 3:10).

Now be still and listen.

MORE READING:

John 10:1–15; 16:5–15

Chapter 6, "Have Courage: The Ache to Hear God" from *The Beautiful Ache* by Leigh McLeroy

A SOUNDTRACK FOR LISTENING:

"And Your Praise Goes On" by Chris Rice

"Let My Words Be Few" by Matt Redman

"Calling Out Your Name" by Rich Mullins

"Wonderful Words of Life" (hymn)

"Let All Mortal Flesh Keep Silence" (hymn)

Perhaps one of the reasons we don't hear Christ's voice more clearly is that he wants to draw us into such a close embrace that the slightest move of his hand against the small of our back tells us all we need to know.[3]

Ken Gire, The Divine Embrace

Exercise 3: Watching

We take in so much of life through our eyes. Jesus himself said that the eye is "the lamp of the body." Our eyes land on things as if a spotlight shone, and what we see evokes emotion: want, fear, longing, dread, desire, and joy. Every now and then we see something unusual or not readily discernable, and we must focus even more intently to consider that thing and identify it.

In the Old Testament we learn that man cannot look on God and live. His holiness is too bright for us; his beauty is too fine. But we have seen the Beautiful One, Jesus, who said that to see him is to see the Father. Poet Emily Dickinson wrote: "The truth must dazzle gradually, or every man be blind!"

Wherever you are right now, close your eyes. Allow yourself to become accustomed to the dark. Now open them again and readjust your vision. Look all around you and take in as much of your surroundings as you are able. What colors do you see? What textures? What movement? What contrasts? Now narrow your vision to a particular object or a smaller scene in the larger scene. What evidence of God do you observe? What emotions does your view evoke? Do you see a person for whom you could pray? A bit of beauty for which you might give thanks? Stop now and respond to God about what your eyes have seen.

Read "The Stereographic View" (p. 109) and "Considering Monovision" (p. 133) in The Sacred Ordinary. Is there something you are striving to see that God has not yet brought into focus? Pray for your sight to stretch to accommodate his vision. Is there something on which your eyes *have* focused to the exclusion of all else? Tell God about that too and ask him to broaden your vistas so that you will not miss all that he has planned for you.

MORE READING:

Revelation 1:20

Acts 9:1–9

Chapter 11, "New Clothes for Cara: The Ache for Beauty" from *The Beautiful Ache* by Leigh McLeroy

A SOUNDTRACK FOR WATCHING:

"Be Thou My Vision" (hymn)

"Open My Eyes That I May See" (hymn)

"My Father's Eyes" by Amy Grant

"What a Wonderful World" by Louis Armstrong

"I Still Haven't Found What I'm Looking For" by U2

We may ignore, but we can nowhere evade, the presence of God. The world is crowded with him.

C. S. Lewis, *Letters to Malcolm: Chiefly on Prayer*

Exercise 4: Hoping

Sometimes God speaks to us through our desires. "Delight yourself in the LORD," wrote the psalmist, "and He will give you the desires of your heart" (Ps. 37:4). Hoping in God is an act of great vulnerability but also one of great intimacy. Many may know our preferences, but only those closest to us know our hopes. A thousand different things can quench hope, but when it is rooted in Christ Jesus, our hope is entirely reasonable!

Spend some time reading "Finding Feathers" (p. 117) and "Finding More Feathers" (p. 118) in *The Sacred Ordinary.* Is there something for which you have long hoped? Imagine that your hope is held not by you, but by another person—someone that you love. What would you tell that person about "their" hope? Would you tell yourself the same thing? Do you believe in God's design for the hopes of others but not for your own?

Write God a letter about your hopes. Tell him why you long for these things. Plead his promises to him regarding your hopes. Confess to him that you are unable to do these things for yourself, and that you need and depend upon him to do them for you. If you can, write this letter by hand—using your "opposite" hand. If you are right-handed, use your left. If you are left-handed, use your right. (Struggling to write somehow overrides the "editor" in all of us and can bring out a surprising, simple honesty. Try it!)

Now, take a look around you or go for a short walk. Being observant of your immediate surroundings, look for things that inspire hope. (An early bloom on a hedge, a baby in a stroller, a full moon.) Take note of these. You might even start a list on your computer of "hope sightings" to read when you are discouraged.

MORE READING:

1 Samuel 1:1–20

Psalm 71:1–14

1 Peter 1:1–9

Chapter 7, "One Bright Red Bird: The Ache of Hope" from *The Beautiful Ache* by Leigh McLeroy

A SOUNDTRACK FOR HOPING:

"The Solid Rock" (hymn)

"Give Me Jesus" by Fernando Ortega

"More" by Andrew Peterson

"Blessed Be Your Name" by Matt Redman

"The Palm of Your Hand" by Allison Krauss

Two types of faith in God are clearly set forth in the Scriptures. One may be called the mind's faith, wherein the intellect assents to a belief that God exists. The other may be referred to as the heart's faith, whereby the whole man is involved in a trusting act of self-surrender. The mind's faith is directed toward a theory, but the heart's faith is centered in a Person.[4]

Martin Luther King Jr.

Exercise 5: Praising

"Praise God!" The words can be heartfelt or hollow. It all depends on you. Plan a time when you can privately praise God. Plan to extol his handiwork (the world), his mighty works on your behalf (the cross, salvation), and his blessings to you this very day. Remember how he has delivered you in the past. Give him honor for his faithfulness to you. Read the psalms of praise below, and let them inspire you to write one of your own. No one else needs to see. It's between you and God.

Consider how you can praise God with everything you are: your lips, your heart, your mind, your hands, and your feet. Change your posture as you praise. Praise is not limited to raised hands or loud drums (although those work!). Lower your body to the ground and lift only your heart to him.

Try a "praise walk." Take a spin around your neighborhood on a bike or on foot. Let the things you see and hear inspire you to praise. Maybe a yard sign that says "It's a girl" will invite you to praise God for a new baby's birth—and your own spiritual birth. Perhaps a school playground will remind you to praise him for the innocence of children and for your position as his adopted child. You get the idea! Because his loving-kindness is everlasting, we should never run out of praise.

C. S. Lewis said that the praise of a good thing is its natural result—that we're not satisfied experiencing any good thing until we've praised it to someone else. So instead of just saying "Praise God," why not share with a friend something God has done for you and say, "I just want to tell you about his goodness to me." Then invite them to do the same.

Read "Never Closed, Never without a Customer" (p. 14) and "Weakness before Wonder" (p. 224) from *The Sacred Ordinary*.

MORE READING:

Psalms 9:1–20; 30:1–12

Luke 1:46–55

Chapter 16, "Singing the Hymnal: The Ache to Worship" from *The Beautiful Ache* by Leigh McLeroy

A SOUNDTRACK FOR PRAISING:

"The Doxology" (hymn)

"Come Thou Fount of Every Blessing" (hymn)

"Better Is One Day" by Charlie Hall

"Lover" by Derek Webb

"Awesome God" by Rich Mullins

I know only enough of God to want to worship him, by any means ready to hand.[5]

Annie Dillard

Notes

Part 1 Ordinary Places

1. Dr. Seuss, *Oh, the Places You'll Go!* (New York: Random House, 1990).

2. Emily Dickinson, *The Complete Poems of Emily Dickinson*, ed. Thomas H. Johnson (New York: Little, Brown, 1997), 1129.

3. George MacDonald, *Diary of an Old Soul: 366 Writings for Devotional Reflection* (Minneapolis: Augsburg, 1994), 101.

Part 2 Ordinary People

1. See www.cbsnews.com/stories/2006/02/23/earlyshow/main1339324.shtml.

2. Dorothy L. Sayers, *Creed or Chaos?* (Manchester, NH: Sophia Institute Press, 1974), 75.

Part 3 Ordinary Things

1. Dickinson, *Complete Poems*, 254.

Part 4 Ordinary Moments

1. Eugene H. Peterson, *Subversive Spirituality* (Grand Rapids: Eerdmans, 1997), 165.

2. Emilie Griffin, *Wilderness Time: A Guide for Spiritual Retreat* (New York: HarperOne, 1997), 33.

3. Flannery O'Connor, "The Fiction Writer and His Country," in *Mystery and Manners: Occasional Prose*, ed. by Sally and Robert Fitzgerald (New York: Farrar, Strauss and Giroux, 1969), 35.

Part 5 Ordinary Words

1. Dickinson, *Complete Poems*, 193.

2. John Piper, *The Pleasures of God: Meditations on God's Delight in Being God* (Sisters, OR: Multnomah, 2000), 281.

3. Michka Assayas, *Bono: In Conversation with Michka Assayas* (New York: Riverhead Books, 2005), 223.

4. G. K. Chesterton, *Orthodoxy* (1908; repr., San Francisco: Ignatius Press, 1995), 81.

5. Annie Dillard, *Teaching a Stone to Talk: Expeditions and Encounters* (New York: Harper Perennial, 1988), 24.

6. Robert McKee, *Story: Substance, Structure, Style, and the Principles of Screenwriting* (New York: HarperCollins, 1997), 317.

Personal Retreat Guide

1. Belden C. Lane, *The Solace of Fierce Landscapes* (New York: Oxford University Press, 1998), 191.

2. Arthur Bennett, *The Valley of Vision: A Collection of Puritan Prayers and Devotions* (Carlisle, PA: Banner of Truth Trust, 1997), 65.

3. Ken Gire, *The Divine Embrace* (Wheaton, IL: Tyndale House, 2003), 132.

4. Martin Luther King Jr., *Strength to Love* (Philadelphia: Fortress Press, 1981), 134.

5. Annie Dillard, *Holy the Firm* (New York: Harper & Row, 1977), 55.

Leigh McLeroy writes and speaks with a passion for God and a keen eye for his presence in everyday life. Leigh is the author of *Moments for Singles*, *The Beautiful Ache*, and *Treasured: Knowing God by the Things He Keeps*. She is also a feature writer whose work has appeared in *Christianity Today*, *Discipleship Journal*, *Prayer*, *Christian Single*, *Radiant*, and *The High Calling of Our Daily Work*. Her e-devotional, Wednesday words has appeared every week since 2003. Connect with Leigh on Facebook, at www.wednesdaywords. com, and www.leighmcleroy.com.